THE DISTRIBUTION OF SPECIES

MICHAEL BRIGHT

Heinemann Library
Chicago, Illinois

Customer service 888-454-2279
Visit our website at www.heinemannraintree.com

Edited by Pollyanna Poulter
Designed by Steven Mead and Q2A Creative Solutions
Illustrated by International Mapping and Sturat Jackson-Carter/The Art Agency
Picture research by Elizabeth Alexander
Production by Alison Parsons
Originated by Dot Gradations
Printed in China by Leo Paper Group

13 12 11 10 09
10 9 8 7 6 5 4 3 2 1

Library of Congress Cataloging-in-Publication Data
Bright, Michael.
  The distribution of species / Michael Bright. -- 1st ed.
    p. cm. -- (Timeline. Life on earth)
  Includes bibliographical references and index.
  ISBN 978-1-4329-1654-1 (hc) -- ISBN 978-1-4329-1660-2 (pb)
  1. Biogcography. I. Title.
  QH84.B747 2008
  577.8--dc22
                        2008019420

Acknowledgments

The Publishers would like to thank the following for permission to reproduce photographs: © 2008 Jupiterimages Corporation: p. **23 top middle** and **middle**; © Alamy: pp. **6** (imagebroker), **25** (Holmes Garden Photos), **33** and **47** (blickwinkel), **36** (Jack Picone); © Brand X Pictures. Morey Milbradt. 2001: p. **14 bottom**; © Corbis: pp. **8** (Tim Davis), **9** (Martin Harvey), **43** (David A. Northcott), **45** (Kevin Schafer); © Digital Vision: p. **29**; © istockphoto: **panel backgrounds** (Elena Schweitzer), **4, 16, 24,** and **40 chapter openers, panel backgrounds, 5** (Jason Maehl), **14 middle** (Weldon Schloneger), **14 top** (Sabrina dei Nobili), **15 bottom** (Robert Bremec), **15 middle** (Edwin van Wier), **15 top** (Morley Read), **19** (Steven Lewarne), **23 bottom, 23 bottom middle** (Chanyut Sribua-rawd), **23 top** (Norma Cornes), **23 main** (Lev Radin); © FLPA: p. **34** (S. Jonasson); © Getty Images: pp. **13** (Cyril Ruoso/JH Editorial), **42** (Bryan Reynolds/Science Faction); © imagequestmarine.com: pp. **10** (Peter Batson), **27** (Valdimar Butterworth).

Cover photograph of African elephant herd walking in line reproduced with permission of © naturepl.com (Karl Ammann), and Earth from space © NASA.

The Publishers would like to thank Mandy Holloway and Gavin Fidler for their invaluable help in the preparation of this book.

Every effort has been made to contact copyright holders of material reproduced in this book. Any omissions will be rectified in subsequent printings if notice is given to the Publishers.

CONTENTS

Some words are printed in bold, **like this**. You can find out what they mean in the glossary.

DISTRIBUTION

Distribution is the geographical range of an **organism**. Plants and animals are not distributed evenly across the globe. Polar bears and lions are both carnivores but live in two distinct parts of the world—polar bears in the Arctic, lions in the Serengeti. Because of this, polar bears and lions are said to have a different distribution. Living organisms can be found wherever there is the prospect of life surviving. It can be at the top of mountains or the bottom of the deepest oceans; in places where it is very dry or very wet, very hot or very cold. Life is found on virtually every part of our planet's surface.

Living at extremes

Most of the living things we see around us inhabit forests, grasslands, mountains, oceans and seas, lakes, and rivers. But life is so adaptable it can survive in the most unexpected places. There are tiny organisms that live sandwiched between thin, translucent layers of rock in the extremely cold, dry valleys of the Antarctic. Deep underground, in South African gold mines, are species of **micro-organisms** that have been isolated from the surface for 20 million years. Miniscule amounts of heat from the decay of uranium and thorium help them survive. Some bacteria live close to boiling hot water vents on the floor of the Pacific Ocean. In the Gulf of Mexico, worms eat bacteria that thrive on

1848
Alfred Russel Wallace and Henry Walter Bates explore Amazon rain forest.

1854
Wallace travels through the islands of the East Indies.

methane hydrate deposits deep down on the seafloor. The colorful hot springs in Yellowstone National Park are the result of bacteria and algae growing in waters that are highly acidic and boiling hot.

Biogeography

Biogeography is the study of the distribution of all these organisms in space and time. It looks at where animals live, why, and how many there are. Naturalist Charles Darwin found out how important this was. His friend, John Gould, noted how the finches on the Galapagos Islands had bills of different shapes depending on which island they lived. They realized there was a link between a species' distribution and its evolution. They began to understand that geography has a big effect on the creation of new species.

New species

Darwin realized that species living on islands are isolated. He also saw that mountains or rivers could split these groups. He could see how newly formed populations adapted to the new conditions around them. Darwin deduced that individuals with traits that help them survive in the new environment reproduce and pass these on to their offspring. Those individuals that do not have features that help them survive die out. Later generations become so different from the original parent population that if individuals from each group met they probably wouldn't be able to reproduce. The new populations would have become new species. This was the basis of Darwin's **theory of evolution** by **natural selection**.

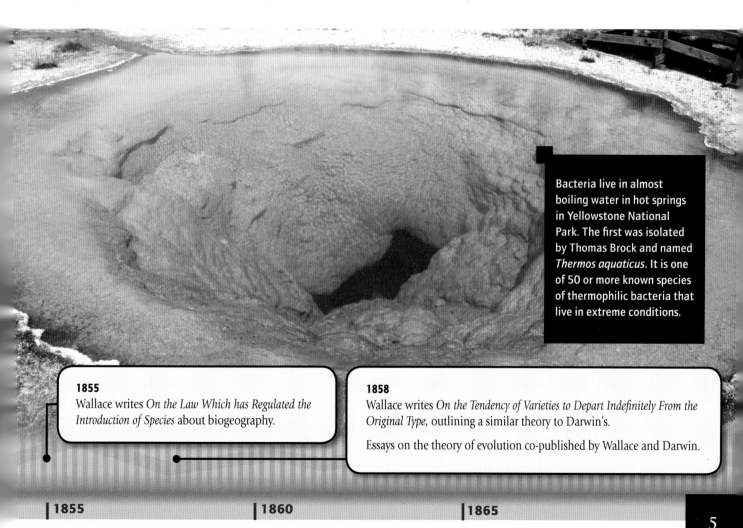

Bacteria live in almost boiling water in hot springs in Yellowstone National Park. The first was isolated by Thomas Brock and named *Thermos aquaticus*. It is one of 50 or more known species of thermophilic bacteria that live in extreme conditions.

1855
Wallace writes *On the Law Which has Regulated the Introduction of Species* about biogeography.

1858
Wallace writes *On the Tendency of Varieties to Depart Indefinitely From the Original Type*, outlining a similar theory to Darwin's.

Essays on the theory of evolution co-published by Wallace and Darwin.

| 1855 | 1860 | 1865

Exclusive!

When a species or family of plants and animals is kept within a particular area and lives nowhere else in the world it is said to be **endemic**. The living space can be an island, **archipelago**, lake, mountain, **plateau**, a type of habitat, county, or a country—any defined area in which the species is unique. Koalas and red kangaroos, for example, are native to Australia; the orange-breasted sunbird is endemic to the fynbos (meaning "fine bush") scrubland in South Africa; the Baikal seal is endemic to Siberia's Lake Baikal; and the Devil's Hole pupfish is exclusive to a single thermal spring on a mountainside in Nevada.

Desert islands

The tropical desert islands of Socotra, off the coast of the Horn of Africa, have many endemic species. They were separated from all continents over 6 million years ago. The geographical isolation and hot, dry climate have resulted in plants and animals (**flora** and **fauna**) quite unique to the islands. The umbrella-shaped dragon's blood tree and the bottle-shaped desert rose are two of 250 plants endemic to Socotra. Fifteen are endemic to the tiny island of Abd al Kuri alone, including a species of *Euphorbia* tree with strange, spineless, column-shaped stems. The main island is just 80 miles (130 km) long and 20 miles (30 km) wide, yet it has its own warbler, bunting, starling, sunbird, sparrow, and grosbeak birds. Twenty-one of its 24 known reptiles are also endemic. If any new plant or animal were introduced it could upset the balance of plants and animals on the islands forever.

EVOLVING AND ADAPTING

- Evolution is a change in the genetic information present in a population of organisms from one generation to the next.
- Adaptation is the adjustment of a species to its environment.

The dragon's blood tree (left) and desert rose (right) are endemic to the tropical island of Socotra. Water droplets, from rain or sea mist, run down the branches of the dragon's blood tree to the stem and roots—an adaptation of living in a hot, dry climate.

Endemic island hotspots

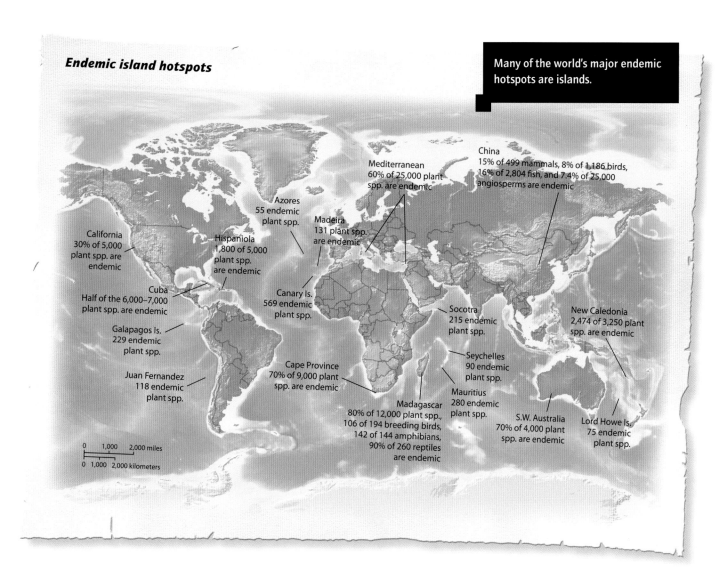

Many of the world's major endemic hotspots are islands.

China
15% of 499 mammals, 8% of 1,186 birds, 16% of 2,804 fish, and 7.4% of 25,000 angiosperms are endemic

Mediterranean
60% of 25,000 plant spp. are endemic

Azores
55 endemic plant spp.

Madeira
131 plant spp. are endemic

California
30% of 5,000 plant spp. are endemic

Hispaniola
1,800 of 5,000 plant spp. are endemic

Cuba
Half of the 6,000–7,000 plant spp. are endemic

Canary Is.
569 endemic plant spp.

Socotra
215 endemic plant spp.

New Caledonia
2,474 of 3,250 plant spp. are endemic

Galapagos Is.
229 endemic plant spp.

Juan Fernandez
118 endemic plant spp.

Cape Province
70% of 9,000 plant spp. are endemic

Seychelles
90 endemic plant spp.

Mauritius
280 endemic plant spp.

Madagascar
80% of 12,000 plant spp., 106 of 194 breeding birds, 142 of 144 amphibians, 90% of 260 reptiles are endemic

S.W. Australia
70% of 4,000 plant spp. are endemic

Lord Howe Is.
75 endemic plant spp.

0   1,000   2,000 miles

0   1,000   2,000 kilometers

Endemism downside

Like all centers of endemism, Socotra's wildlife is at risk if there are any changes. Settlers on the islands brought goats with them. The expanding population of these animals eats just about anything, including the new shoots of endemic plants. The habitat has also been fragmented by excessive woodcutting for timber and fuel, leaving small, vulnerable patches of surviving vegetation. It has led conservationists to put Socotra in the top ten of the world's most threatened floras. The main problem for endemic species is the restricted habitat. If anything should change, such as a shift in the climate or the introduction of alien species, then endemic species would find it hard to cope. All over the world, the influence of human activities and rapidly changing conditions mean that endemic species are often endangered.

ISLANDS EXPLAINED

- An island is an isolated piece of land surrounded entirely by water. Ireland, in Europe, is an island.
- An archipelago is a chain or group of islands. The Galapagos Islands off the coast of Ecuador are an archipelago.
- An atoll is an island of coral that surrounds a lagoon. Midway Atoll in the Pacific is an atoll on top of an extinct volcano.

All over the world

Animals that live in many parts of the world are said to have a **cosmopolitan** distribution. For example, the house dust mite is found all over the world. The brown rat has spread from its native habitat in northern China by human transportation, and is now found almost everywhere on the planet. Likewise, the **feral** pigeon, a domesticated version of the Eurasian rock pigeon, has been introduced widely and is now common throughout the world. Humans are a cosmopolitan species and wherever we go, other species follow, especially **parasites**. The pork and beef tapeworms, for example, have a cosmopolitan distribution because of us.

Same habitat worldwide

Cosmopolitan can literally mean "global." In biogeography, it usually refers to plants or animals that only live in a particular habitat found in many parts of the world. The sea has many cosmopolitan species.

Orcas, or killer whales, are found in all the world's oceans, from the tropics to the poles. The humpback whale prefers to live in waters close to shore, breeding in the tropics and feeding in **temperate** and polar seas. Separate populations live in the Indian, Atlantic, and Pacific oceans. Those in the southern hemisphere rarely encounter those in the north because the seasons are out of step. Nevertheless, its distribution is said to be cosmopolitan.

Great white sharks inhabit temperate and sub-tropical seas, both in coastal waters and the open ocean. At certain times of the year, they stay where their main prey (seals and sea lions) breed, such as California, South Africa, and Chile in South America. Some sharks even move between major population centers. Female sharks have even been found to travel back and forth across the Indian Ocean between South Africa and Western Australia! Great whites have a cosmopolitan distribution.

Great white sharks live part of their lives close to shore and part in the open ocean. They are found in all of the world's oceans, except polar waters, making them a cosmopolitan species.

Feral pigeons are found in most cities in the world, making them a cosmopolitan species. The world pigeon population is expected to rise to 400 million during the next decade.

Extreme north and south

The more scientists explore the world of extremely small organisms, the more surprises they find. As part of the British Antarctic Survey, David Pierce, together with colleagues at Uppsala University, Sweden, and the Open University, in the United Kingdom, has been studying **DNA** from bacteria living in freshwater lakes in the Arctic and Antarctic. They have discovered that the same groups of bacteria dominate lakes at both ends of the world. It is new evidence that lends support to the global ubiquity **hypothesis** of micro-organisms. This theory states there are so many micro-organisms that are so easily spread they have a cosmopolitan distribution. They grow anywhere in conditions that suit them; in other words "everything is everywhere."

UNEXPECTED HABITATS

The dust mite is a tiny bug related to spiders. It is only 150 **microinches** long, so it can barely be seen even with a magnifying glass! It lives in our houses and feeds on the dead skin cells from humans. Its partially digested food and waste cause allergic reactions in some people and are a common cause of asthma. It is found wherever people live all over the world.

Tapeworms are parasitic flatworms that live in the intestines of animals. The adult stage consists of a head that anchors the tapeworm in place and a body made up of many reproductive segments joined together. A tapeworm can be up to 30 ft. (10 meters) long!

Biogeographical regions

In 1628, Robert Burton wrote in his *The Anatomy of Melancholy*:

"Why doth Africa breed so many venomous beasts, Ireland none … whence comes this variety of complexions, colours, plants, birds, beasts, metals, peculiar to every place?"

Burton was one of many explorers to notice that places separated by geographical features (such as oceans, deserts, and mountain chains) have different faunas and floras. By the 19th century, **naturalists** had enough information to draw up maps dividing the world into distinct **zoogeographic** regions. These are regions of the world containing distinct species of animals. In 1858, **ornithologist** Philip L. Sclater used divisions based on the distribution of bird species, recognizing both the Old World and the New World. He divided the Old World into: Europe and northern Asia; Africa south of the Sahara; India and southern Asia; Australia and New Guinea, and the New World into North and South America. In 1876, Alfred Russel Wallace (see page 12) revised Sclater's map to create six zoogeographical realms: Nearctic; Neotropical; Palearctic; Ethiopian; Oriental; and Australian. It is a **classification** still in use today.

OLD AND NEW WORLDS

- The Old World is the world that was known to Europeans, Africans, and Asians in the 15th century before Christopher Columbus came to the Americas.
- The New World generally refers to North, Central, and South America, areas of the world that were new to Europeans.

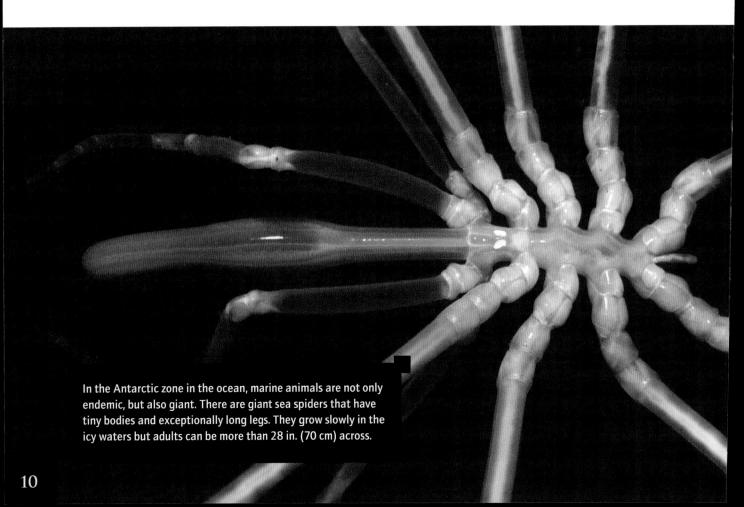

In the Antarctic zone in the ocean, marine animals are not only endemic, but also giant. There are giant sea spiders that have tiny bodies and exceptionally long legs. They grow slowly in the icy waters but adults can be more than 28 in. (70 cm) across.

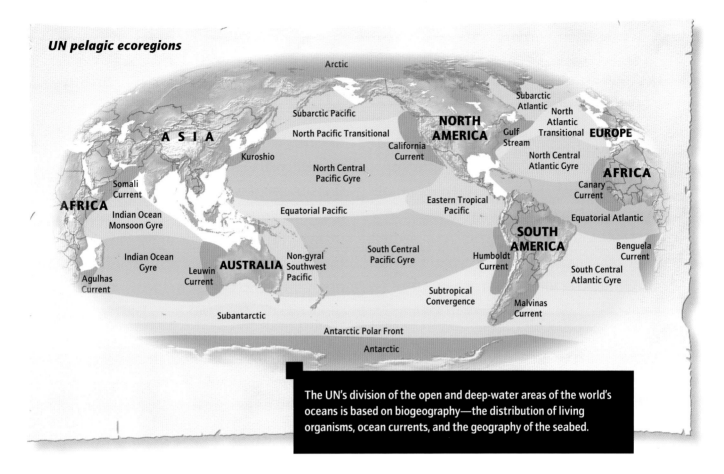

UN pelagic ecoregions

Arctic

Subarctic Pacific

North Pacific Transitional

ASIA

Kuroshio

Somali
Current

AFRICA

Indian Ocean
Monsoon Gyre

California
Current

North Central
Pacific Gyre

Equatorial Pacific

NORTH
AMERICA

Subarctic
Atlantic North
Atlantic
Gulf Transitional **EUROPE**
Stream

North Central
Atlantic Gyre

AFRICA

Canary
Current

Eastern Tropical
Pacific

Equatorial Atlantic

SOUTH
AMERICA

Indian Ocean
Gyre

Agulhas
Current

AUSTRALIA

Leuwin
Current

Non-gyral
Southwest
Pacific

South Central
Pacific Gyre

Humboldt
Current

Benguela
Current

South Central
Atlantic Gyre

Subtropical
Convergence

Malvinas
Current

Subantarctic

Antarctic Polar Front

Antarctic

The UN's division of the open and deep-water areas of the world's oceans is based on biogeography—the distribution of living organisms, ocean currents, and the geography of the seabed.

Similarity index

In order to draw up these maps, biogeographers look for the number of species, or groups of species, that are similar in each region. Take mammals, for example. In New Guinea and Australia they are 93 percent similar. This suggests there is a close relationship between the two areas. In New Guinea and the islands of the Caribbean they are only 21 percent similar. This indicates that these two areas are far apart both geographically and zoologically.

Modern interpretations

The Sclater-Wallace maps are still used for life on land. Advances in **oceanography** and marine biology have meant that similar biogeographical maps can be drawn up for life in the sea.

There are many versions but a nine-zone division is generally used:

- Arctic and Antarctic zones
- sub-Arctic and sub-Antarctic zones
- north and south temperate or transition zones
- north and south sub-tropical zones
- the tropical zone.

These can be subdivided in many different ways. In June 2007, at a meeting of United Nations agencies, the open sea and deep ocean was divided into 29 provinces. These were based on factors such as ocean currents and areas of upwellings, where nutrients from the deep sea are brought to the surface. Recognizing these divisions and the differences in flora and fauna is important so we can manage and conserve the oceans.

ALFRED RUSSEL WALLACE (1823–1913)

Welsh naturalist and explorer Alfred Russel Wallace was the "father of biogeography." He lived at the same time as Charles Darwin. Through his fieldwork in the Malay Archipelago he came to the same conclusion as Darwin: that natural selection is the driving force behind evolution. Wallace and Darwin's essays on this subject were both presented on July 1, 1858, at the Linnean Society in London, England.

Wallace's line

Despite his contribution to evolutionary theory, Wallace is better known for his biogeographical fieldwork in southern Asia. After a stint in the Amazon, he traveled extensively in Indonesia. He undertook more than 70 expeditions in eight years and collected 125,660 specimens, of which more than 1,000 were new to science. He also noticed that plants and animals in the east of Indonesia tended to have Australasian origins, whereas those in the west were more closely linked to Asia. Wallace drew an imaginary line through the region. He thought that plants and animals to the west of the line came mainly from Asia and those to the east of the line came mainly from Australia.

This pattern of distribution on either side of Wallace's line is based on ancient sea levels. The line follows the position of a deepwater channel between the Sunda and

Wallace, Weber's, and Lydekker's lines

▼ These lines follow natural channels that were filled with water even when the sea level dropped during the Ice Ages. This prevented plants and animals from passing between islands.

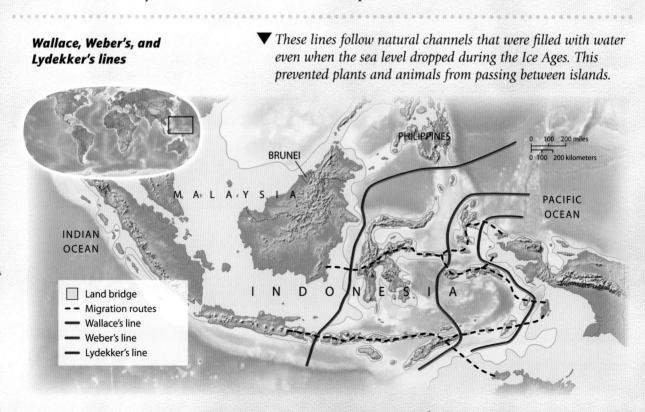

PHILIPPINES

BRUNEI

MALAYSIA

INDIAN OCEAN

PACIFIC OCEAN

INDONESIA

0   100   200 miles
0   100   200 kilometers

□ Land bridge
-- Migration routes
— Wallace's line
— Weber's line
— Lydekker's line

PRESENTING ESSAYS

In 1858, when the essays of Darwin and Wallace were presented to the Linnean Society, Wallace was collecting animals in Borneo and Darwin was mourning the death of one of his children. As was common practice at the time, the Secretary of the Society, John Joseph Bennett, carried out the reading of the papers. President of the Society, Thomas Bell, chaired the meeting at which about 30 people were present. The room in which the essays were read is in Old Burlington House, off Piccadilly, London—currently home to the Royal Academy of Arts. A plaque on the wall commemorates the event.

Sahul shelves. Millions of years ago, sea levels were lower and the string of islands on either side of the line were joined together. But there was still a deep-water channel dividing the islands. Wallace thought this channel had prevented Asian species from moving further east and Australasian species from moving west.

Weber and Lydekker's lines

Not all biologists agreed with the position of Wallace's line. In 1902, the Dutch **zoologist** Max Weber (1852–1937) felt that the Indonesian island of Sulawesi (then called Celebes) was closer biologically and geologically to Asia. He also recognized that the Moluccan islands are at the far west of the Australia–New Guinea continental shelf. So Weber drew his line further to the east. More recently, scientists think the region between Weber and Wallace's lines is a transitional zone, which means that it has a mix of species from both continents and is a recognized **biodiversity hotspot**. This area is called Wallacea, in Wallace's honor.

A third boundary—Lydekker's line—was placed further to the east again. English naturalist and geologist Richard Lydekker (1849–1915) established the line in 1895. It marks a more easterly boundary between Wallacea and New Guinea–Australia, and is considered to be the eastern limit of Asia's flora.

▲ *The lesser bird of paradise lives in the tropical forests of Papua New Guinea. Here, many plants and animals are more closely related to those in Australia than those in Asia.*

EARTH'S MAJOR BIOMES

The world's major plant and animal groups can also be divided into **biomes**. There are six main types:

- grassland
- forest
- tundra
- marine
- freshwater
- desert

The classification is based on the main types of vegetation found in each biome and on the adaptations of the organisms that live there.

Grassland

Savannah Tropical grassland, with wet and dry seasons. Soils are porous so rain absorbs quickly. Rainfall is 20–50 in. (50–127 cm) per year. There can be different species of grass depending on the soil. Flora includes scattered trees. Fauna includes antelope, giraffes, kangaroos, lions, cheetahs, hyenas, and elephants.

Temperate The soil is fertile and grasses dominate. There are few trees or large shrubs. Examples are: the steppe of Russia; pampas of Argentina; prairies of North America. There are hot summers and cold winters. Fauna includes prairie dogs, coyotes, and grouse.

Tundra

Arctic The Arctic tundra encircles the Arctic and south, to the great boreal forests, the taiga. It has a layer of **permafrost** soil. There is a short summer and a growing season of 50–60 days. Frozen during winter with bogs and ponds in summer. Flora includes low shrubs and sedges, flowers, and lichens. Fauna includes lemmings, caribou, arctic foxes, ravens, loons, and mosquitoes.

Alpine Found high on mountains. It has well drained soil and a growing season of about 180 days. Flora includes tussock grasses, dwarf trees, and shrubs. Fauna includes marmots, mountain goats, ptarmigan, and deer.

Freshwater

Lakes and ponds Ponds are sometimes seasonal. Lakes last for hundreds of years. Limited diversity of species due to isolation. Divided into zones:

- near the shore is the topmost littoral zone with algae, aquatic insects, fish, and amphibians
- the open water limnetic zone is dominated by plankton and fish
- the bottom profundal zone is occupied by scavengers.

Rivers and streams Water flowing quickly in one direction contains high oxygen levels near its source, with fish (e.g. trout). Mid-river is wider and slower with more diverse flora and fauna, including aquatic green plants. River mouth is murkier, due to sediments and low oxygen. Fish include catfish and carp.

Wetlands Made up of standing water, such as marshes, swamps, and bogs. High level of biodiversity. Flora includes cattails, sedges, and cypress. Fauna includes amphibians and birds, such as ducks and shorebirds.

Forest

Tropical Rainforests are home to the greatest biodiversity on Earth. The 12-hour day varies little all year but there are dry and wet seasons. Rainfall can be more than 80 in. (200 cm) per year. Poor soil since plant nutrients are locked up in the fabric of trees. Trees can be 200 ft. (61 m) tall and are covered with plants such as bromeliads, orchids, and lianas. Fauna includes monkeys, birds, bats, and millions of insect species. There are four layers:

- floor (home to fauna like agoutis and jaguars)
- understory (home to fauna like nectar-feeding bats and hummingbirds)
- canopy (home to fauna like monkeys and parrots)
- emergents (home to fauna like harpy eagles and courting butterflies)

Temperate Clearly defined seasons with rainfall evenly distributed throughout the year. The forests of New England, western Europe, Tasmania, and South-central Chile are temperate. Made up of broad-leaved trees that lose their leaves in winter, such as oak, beech, and maple. Soil is fertile and decaying wood provides food for many species of fungi. Fauna includes squirrels, deer, timber wolf, and black bears.

Boreal (taiga) Largest **terrestrial** biome, found between 50° and 60° latitude. Thick canopy means little light in the understory. Made up of cold-tolerant trees with needle-like leaves, such as pines, firs, and spruces. Fauna includes grizzly bears, moose, lynx, and wolves.

Marine

Oceans Make up the world's largest ecosystem. Divided into zones:

- intertidal zone—exposed and submerged with the tides
- pelagic zone—the open ocean
- abyssal zone—the deep sea
- benthic zone—the bottom of the sea.

Coral reefs Found in warm, shallow seas as barriers along coasts, fringing islands, or as atolls (see page 7). The world's largest is the Great Barrier Reef, Australia. Corals dominate, along with fish including sharks, starfish, sea urchins, and octopuses.

Estuaries Occur where freshwater merges with saltwater. Flora includes seaweeds, mangroves, and marsh grasses. Fauna includes worms, oysters, crabs, and shorebirds.

Desert

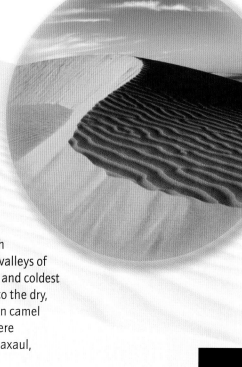

Hot and dry Hot in summer with little rain. The central Sahara desert in Africa receives 0.6 in. (1.5 cm) rain per year. Flora often have thick leaves to reduce water loss and include ground-hugging plants, woody trees, and succulent plants such as yucca, cacti, and agaves. Fauna is mainly nocturnal and burrowing, to hide from the heat. It includes insects, scorpions, reptiles, and kangaroo rats.

Semi-arid Found in the Australian outback and western part of the North and South Dakota. Known as sagebrush deserts in the United States because sagebrush is the main plant living there. Flora includes creosote bush and mesquite, and often has spines and hairs to reduce water loss and glossy leaves to reflect heat. Fauna follows the shade to stay cool and includes jackrabbits, skunks, lizards, snakes, and burrowing owls.

Coastal Deserts alongside the sea. Plenty of water moisture from ocean fogs and mists that flora and fauna are adapted to collect. The Namib of southwest Africa is a coastal desert. It has a Namib beetle that stands on its head so water condensing on its body runs into its mouth. The most bizarre plant in the Namib is Welwitschia, a shrub that grows two, long, strap-shaped leaves and absorbs water.

Cold Experiences cold winters with snow, and warm summers. The dry valleys of the Antarctic are among the driest and coldest places on Earth. Fauna is adapted to the dry, cold conditions, such as the Bactrian camel of the Gobi desert in Mongolia, where vegetation is sparse, and includes saxaul, wormwood, and beancaper.

WHY LIVING THINGS ARE
WHERE THEY ARE

In ecological biogeography every species is said to occupy an ecological niche. It is more than simply a place. U.S. ecologist W. Bruce Saunders, at Bryn Mawr College, Pennsylvania, says it depends "not only on where the species lives, but what it does." For example, a humpback whale lives most of its life near the shore; feeds on fish and krill which it sieves from the water; interacts with others of its kind; migrates huge distances across the ocean; and is harassed by killer whales. All of these things describe its ecological niche.

One of the competitors will gain an advantage over the other until one is either driven to extinction or forced to make an evolutionary shift into a different niche. For example, two whale species could have been competing for fish close to shore. One developed longer flippers, like the humpback, and became skilled at catching fish. The other changed very little and was less successful at feeding. Eventually the disadvantaged whale became extinct, leaving the humpback to fill the ecological niche available for that type of whale.

Competing for a niche

Two species seldom occupy the same niche for long because they compete against each other.

Sharing resources

Species competing for the same food source can sometimes live alongside each other

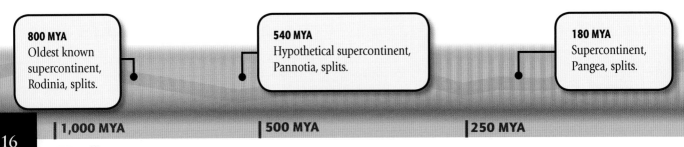

800 MYA
Oldest known supercontinent, Rodinia, splits.

540 MYA
Hypothetical supercontinent, Pannotia, splits.

180 MYA
Supercontinent, Pangea, splits.

| 1,000 MYA

| 500 MYA

| 250 MYA

MYA = million years ago

by sharing that resource. In the Caribbean, several species of *Anolis* lizards live in the same tropical rain forest and eat the same kind of food, mainly insects. They share this resource by living in different parts of the forest. One species hunts on the forest floor, another in the understory, and a third in the canopy. This means that they don't have to compete with each other directly.

Fundamental and realized niches

Species occupy a fundamental niche and a realized niche. A species' fundamental niche depends on a range of conditions, such as temperature, humidity, and rainfall. A plant or animal that does well in a Mediterranean climate, for example, need not be restricted to the Mediterranean. The same climate is found elsewhere in the world, especially on the western coasts of continental landmasses, such as in California, South Africa, southwest Australia, and central Chile. The vegetation in each of these places is very similar—maquis in the Mediterranean, chaparral in California, fynbos in South Africa, matorral in Chile, and mallee in Australia. In theory, a Mediterranean-type organism could live in any of those places.

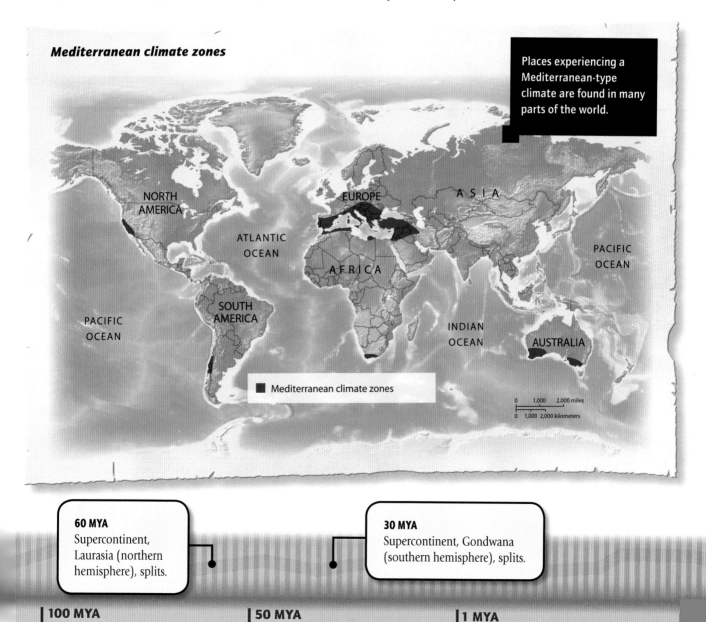

Mediterranean climate zones

Places experiencing a Mediterranean-type climate are found in many parts of the world.

■ Mediterranean climate zones

0   1,000   2,000 miles
0 1,000 2,000 kilometers

60 MYA
Supercontinent, Laurasia (northern hemisphere), splits.

30 MYA
Supercontinent, Gondwana (southern hemisphere), splits.

| 100 MYA | 50 MYA | 1 MYA |

VARIED VEGETATIONS

Maquis—scrubland in the Mediterranean
Chaparral—scrubland in California
Fynbos—scrubland in South Africa
Matorral—scrubland in Spain
Mallee—scrubland and woodland
in Australia

Species, however, also interact with others. These interactions, such as competition with rivals and the impact of predators on prey, generally force a species into a more specific niche, one to which it is better adapted than any other **organism**. This is the species' realized niche. Joseph H. Connell at the University of California in Santa Barbara, studied two species of barnacle. Both species evolved to live on the rocky shore—their fundamental niche. One species, which was able to keep from drying out and survived predation by sea snails better than the other, could live on the more exposed rock surfaces. This was its realized niche.

Long term studies

Historical biogeography examines the origins and evolutionary history of species on a much longer time scale than ecological biogeography. Historical biogeography uses evidence from the study of fossils (**paleontology**) and molecular biology.

AREA CLADOGRAMS

Area cladograms enable historical biogeographers to track the evolutionary history of an organism and determine how differences in the environment have influenced the evolution of different species with a common origin. Essentially, these are "family trees" with the species name replaced by the geographic location in which it lives. The evolutionary relationships between species and the places where they live are shown.

These diagrams show five species in four locations. All share the same ancestor—"common ancestor." Each joint in the cladogram represents the moment a new species evolved. The cladogram on the left shows the relationship of the five species and by what route each evolved. In the area cladogram on the right, each species has been replaced by its geographical location. Scientists can use diagrams like these to determine whether a new species arose because a barrier separated their ancestors, or it simply dispersed from one area to the next.

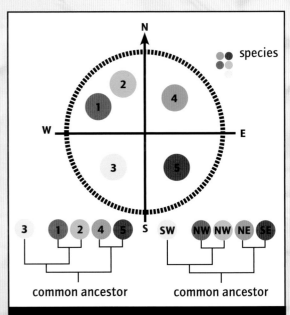

Cladogram of the evolutionary relationships (above left) and biogeographical relationships (above right) of five different species in four different locations.

Gardeners can tell you that many modern ferns do well in shady areas. This is because many millions of years ago, their ancestors thrived in the shadow of rapidly evolving trees.

Fossils provide information about where plants and animals used to live—their past distribution. In molecular biology, molecular clocks—molecules that change over time—help show how species were related and what their relationship is now. The information is used to find out where an organism started; how it arrived at the place we see it today and by what route; how a community of animals came to be assembled; and the barriers that limited its spread or dispersal. Historical biogeography also helps scientists understand patterns of distribution that **ecology** alone fails to explain.

Ferns versus angiosperms

One of the botanical mysteries studied by biogeographers is the ongoing competition between **angiosperms** and ferns. It has been generally thought that the rise of the flowering plants during the Cretaceous period, about 144 million years ago, resulted in a drop in the diversity of ferns. In short, ferns once dominated the land but their position was taken over by the flowering plants. The feeling among botanists was that modern ferns were organisms left over from better times. A more recent study questions that view.

In 2003, Kathleen Pryer and her colleagues at Duke University in North Carolina, examined fossil ferns and analyzed the **DNA** of living ferns to reveal a very different scenario. Instead of taking a back seat, the ferns actually took advantage of new ecological niches created by trees. They thrived in the localized climate, or microclimate, found in the shade of trees. Many new species of ferns appeared. Some of the ancient fern species still survive in tropical forests, but they are greatly outnumbered by the new ferns. Today, there are 10,000 living species!

ALFRED WEGENER AND CONTINENTAL DRIFT

German scientist Alfred Wegener (1880–1930) was trained in astronomy and had a career in meteorology, but he studied a number of different sciences. This enabled him to look at subjects from many points of view. In 1911, while browsing the library at the University of Marburg, he noticed that certain geological features were similar on both sides of the Atlantic Ocean. He saw that if Africa and South America were placed next to each other, they fit like a jigsaw puzzle. Further north, the coalfields in Europe lined up with those in North America. Fossils on each continent matched, too. Wegener saw that fossils of a prehistoric **reptile**, *Mesosaurus*, were found in southern Africa and eastern South America. As freshwater species, they were unlikely to have crossed the Atlantic. He thought something else must be responsible for the puzzling distribution.

Gondwana fossils ▶

About 180 million years ago, the supercontinent Pangea split first into a southern supercontinent, Gondwana, and a northern supercontinent, Laurasia. They, in turn, split into the continents as we see them today. The distribution of fossils of flora and fauna that lived on Gondwana indicates how the present continents in the southern hemisphere (except India which is in the northern hemisphere) might have fit together previously.

MESOSAURUS

Reptiles evolved from amphibians, leaving the water about 370 million years ago, during the Devonian period. *Mesosaurus* lived about 290 million years ago, during the early Permian. It made its home in freshwater lakes and ponds and was one of the first reptiles to return to water to live. Its feet were webbed and its tail had a fin. Its long hind legs were probably used to propel it through the water. *Mesosaurus* found an unexploited source of food and living space in freshwater, so it reversed the trend to be a **terrestrial** reptile and became an aquatic one instead.

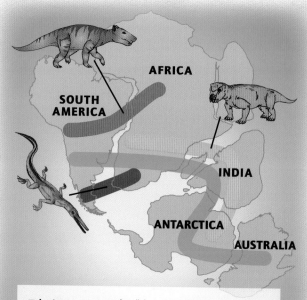

- *Lystrosaurus*, meaning "shovel reptile", was a pig-sized plant-eater
- *Cynognathus*, meaning "dog jaw" was a predatory, mammal-like reptile
- *Mesosaurus* was an aquatic reptile
- *Glossopteris* is an extinct fern species with tongue-shaped leaves

Supercontinent

The more Wegener read, the more he was convinced that about 250 million years ago there had been a supercontinent. He called this Pangea and suggested it had split up and its various parts "drifted" into the positions we see today. In 1915, he published his theory of continental drift. The theory was met with skepticism because he failed to find a mechanism that would cause the continents to drift around on the surface of the Earth. It was largely ignored for more than 30 years. Wegener, in the meantime, had died prematurely while working in Greenland.

A mechanism

In the 1960s, the idea of continental drift resurfaced. Harry Hess, at Princeton University in New Jersey, showed that magma—molten rock that forms below the Earth's surface—oozes up through gashes in the ocean floor. These are the mid-oceanic ridges, such as the Mid-Atlantic Ridge. The new ocean floor spreads on either side of the ridge. As the sea floor moves—known as sea floor spreading—it carries the continents with it. They are, in effect, floating, and the mechanism causing it to happen is convection currents. These are the same currents that you see in a beaker of colored water that is being warmed from below. The warm water rises, cools, and then sinks on either side of the warm column. When it reaches the bottom it warms up and the cycle starts all over again. The same thing occurs in the upper parts of the Earth's mantle, the heat coming from the center of the Earth. Hess, then, had found a way to explain Wegener's theory. The work formed the basis of what is now called **plate tectonics**. It is a theory that has enabled biologists and paleontologists to explain some of the more puzzling cases of plant and animal distribution across the planet (see also pages 22–23).

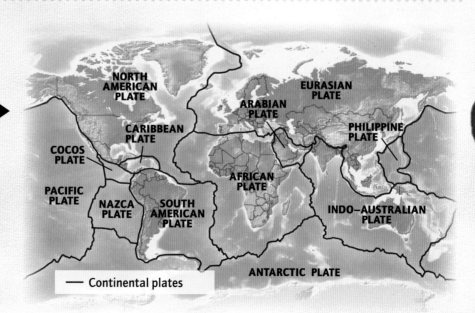

Continental plates today ▶

The map shows Earth's major continental plate boundaries. The continental plates are 25–31 miles (40–50 km) thick and made of silica-rich rocks. The oceanic plates made of basaltic rocks are just 3–4 miles (6–7 km) thick. They move at 0.5–4 in. (1–10 cm) per year.

NORTH AMERICAN PLATE
EURASIAN PLATE
ARABIAN PLATE
CARIBBEAN PLATE
PHILIPPINE PLATE
COCOS PLATE
PACIFIC PLATE
AFRICAN PLATE
NAZCA PLATE
SOUTH AMERICAN PLATE
INDO–AUSTRALIAN PLATE
ANTARCTIC PLATE

— Continental plates

RELICT SPECIES

A relict species is the remnant of a family that once had a wider distribution. Ancestors of New Zealand's tuatara, a primitive lizard-like reptile, had their heyday about 200 million years ago. They were a group of reptiles that occupied many of the ecological niches held today by modern lizards. The tuatara itself was adapted to the cold, so when other reptile species pushed out the tuatara's warm-weather relatives, the tuatara itself survived in lands closer to the poles, such as the islands of New Zealand. Polynesian rats were later introduced to the islands by settlers. The rats killed young tuataras, so today tuataras are confined only to a handful of offshore islands.

Separated by time and space

A marsupial female mammal rears her young in a pouch. Today, marsupials live in Australia and North and South America and fossil marsupials are found in the rocks of Antarctica. Similarly, large, flightless birds—known as ratites—are found on three widely separated continents. The African ostrich, Australia's emu and cassowary, South America's rhea and tinamou, New Zealand's kiwi and extinct moa, and Madagascar's extinct elephant bird all live (or are found as fossils) many thousands of miles apart. This distribution of widely separated but related species is known as disjunct distribution. Disjunction is generally caused by natural events, such as continental drift or climate change.

Geological change

The distribution of the marsupials and ratites was the result of large-scale geological change. In the southern hemisphere, geological disjunctions are common where the present continents were once joined together as the southern supercontinent Gondwana. When it began to split, plants and animals either sat tight on the section they were living on or migrated into whichever part they happened to be close to. The continents drifted apart and today we find them widely separated, as living animals or as fossils.

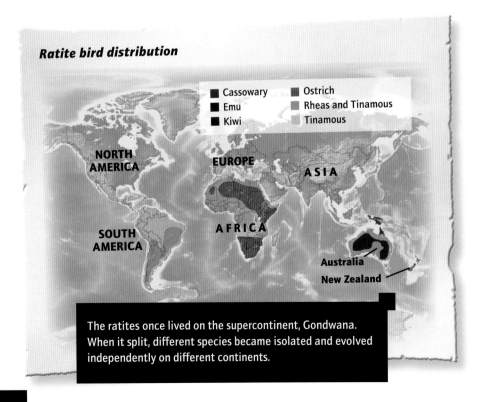

Ratite bird distribution

Cassowary
Emu
Kiwi
Ostrich
Rheas and Tinamous
Tinamous

NORTH AMERICA
EUROPE
ASIA
SOUTH AMERICA
AFRICA
Australia
New Zealand

The ratites once lived on the supercontinent, Gondwana. When it split, different species became isolated and evolved independently on different continents.

Climate change

Magnolia and tulip trees have a disjunct distribution. There are pockets of them in the Old and New World with no apparent link. This disjunction was the result of climate changes. Once, these trees dominated forests across the northern hemisphere, including Greenland. During the Ice Age, they were pushed south, ahead of the great ice sheets that covered much of the northern hemisphere. They grew in more southerly lands, closer to the equator. Some parts of the population became isolated from others and their geographical range fragmented. When the ice retreated, the trees failed to return north to their former distribution. Today, the populations that remain—tulip trees in China and the eastern United States and magnolias in southern Asia and the Americas—are widely separated.

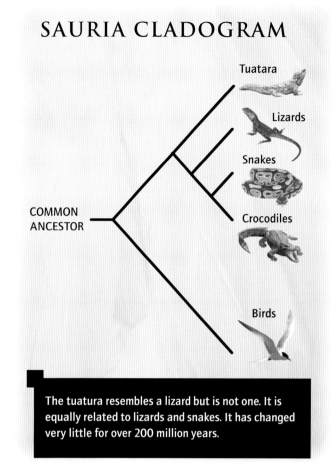

SAURIA CLADOGRAM

Tuatara

Lizards

Snakes

Crocodiles

Birds

COMMON ANCESTOR

The tuatura resembles a lizard but is not one. It is equally related to lizards and snakes. It has changed very little for over 200 million years.

ANCIENT TREES TODAY

Magnolias and tulip trees were among the first flowering plants to appear during the Cretaceous period, about 90 million years ago. In North America, the trunk of tulip trees was used for making lightweight, dugout canoes. In Europe, magnolias have become popular garden plants, and one of the first trees to flower in early spring.

SPREADING FROM PLACE TO PLACE

Dispersal is the process by which an **organism** maintains its existing population or expands its population and moves into a new area.

Population maintenance

A parent organism reduces any competition with itself by making sure its offspring move some distance away. The seeds of flowering plants, **spores** of fungi, and the free-floating larvae of crabs do this. The ways in which they disperse vary from species to species. Many plants simply cast their spores or seeds to the wind. Some have adaptations to help them go further. Eurasian dandelion seeds have hairy parachutes; maple seeds are like miniature helicopters; tree-of-heaven seeds spin like a rolling pin; and the large seeds of the Asian climbing gourd have wings resembling a stealth bomber that help it glide in a great circle around the parent tree. Web-building spiders take to the air, too. Like a plant, the adult spider tends to stay in one place. It sits in its web, and does not venture far. But its babies (spiderlings) use the wind to move away. They each spin a silken line that carries them away, a behavior known as ballooning.

Exploding and squirting

Some plants explode! If you sit next to a gorse bush on a hot summer's day, you can hear the seedpods rip apart as seeds are flung away. Other plants squirt. The squirting cucumber

70–65 MYA	31.5 MYA	25 MYA
Marsupials travel from South America through Antarctica to Australia.	Cavimorph rodents island-hop from Africa to South America.	Monkeys island-hop from Africa to South America.

75 MYA   **50 MYA**   **25 MYA**

MYA = million years ago

releases its seeds in a powerful jet of water. Water, in the form of raindrops, falls into the cup of the bird's nest fungus, the force of the splash pushing out packets of spores. And, the coconut palm produces a fibrous fruit (a drupe) that floats away on the ocean currents to distant lands.

Co-evolution

Animals help some plants. The plants produce mouth-watering fruits, berries, and nuts that animals, such as monkeys, cannot resist. If the seed is swallowed whole, it passes through the animal's digestive system. It is then left some distance from the parent tree, complete with a drop of fertilizer to help it germinate. In the Amazon, even fish eat fruit and nuts. Relatives of the notorious piranha wait in the water under trees for nuts to fall.

Insurance policy

By dispersing its offspring in these ways an organism not only reduces competition but also ensures its population occupies and makes full use of the habitat. The population has access to as much of the available resources as possible, insurance in case things take a turn for the worse.

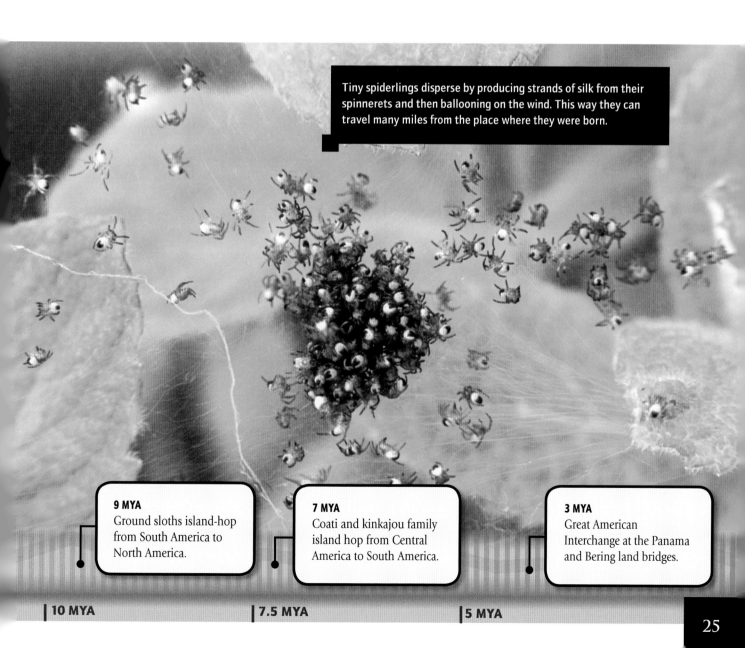

Tiny spiderlings disperse by producing strands of silk from their spinnerets and then ballooning on the wind. This way they can travel many miles from the place where they were born.

9 MYA
Ground sloths island-hop from South America to North America.

7 MYA
Coati and kinkajou family island hop from Central America to South America.

3 MYA
Great American Interchange at the Panama and Bering land bridges.

| 10 MYA

| 7.5 MYA

| 5 MYA

WHALE ISLANDS

Dispersal mechanisms not only make sure an organism is making full use of its current habitat, but also give it the opportunity to explore new places. Most animals are able to walk, swim, or fly and plants have their seeds or spores. Some creatures, however, are so specialized it is hard to see how they can disperse away from their current living place. So how do they do it?

Home base

About 7,000 ft. (2,100 m) down on the bottom of the ocean, in some parts of the world, are self-contained communities of animals. They live close to hot springs under the sea called deep-sea hydrothermal vents. The water temperature can be as high as 750°F (400°C), yet the water does not boil since it is under great pressure. At the bottom of this food chain are bacteria that convert hydrogen sulphide in the hot water into food. All the other animals depend on them. In vents in the Pacific there are giant clams and mussels, squat lobsters, white crabs, and tube worms more than 6.6 ft. (2 m) long. Eyeless shrimp are found beside vents in the Atlantic. It is a community thriving on energy from the center of the Earth, rather than from the sun. Vents, however, do not pump hot water forever. Eventually, they turn off.

Deep study

For marine biologists, this has raised a big question. How does the whole community move to another vent, which may be many miles away under the sea? One of those scientists is Craig Smith at the University of Hawaii, and he has come up with an unexpected answer. He believes that when the carcasses of dead baleen whales sink into the deep sea, they become biological stepping-stones. These enable at least some of these deep-sea creatures to **colonize** fresh habitats.

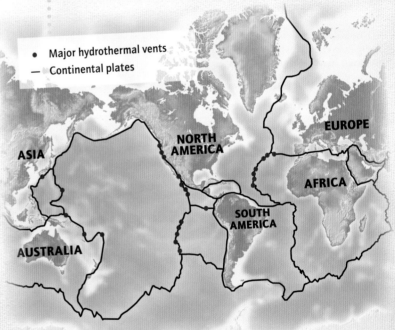

- Major hydrothermal vents
- Continental plates

ASIA
NORTH AMERICA
EUROPE
AFRICA
SOUTH AMERICA
AUSTRALIA

▲ *Deep-sea hydrothermal vents*
Deep-sea hydrothermal vents are geysers on the sea floor. Most are found in areas where the sea floor spreads at mid-oceanic ridges. These ridges are a result of the underwater mountain chain that winds its way through the world's oceans.

Islands in the deep sea

Evidence of vent animals on whale carcasses was first found in 1987. Smith and his co-workers were in the research submarine *Alvin* on the seafloor in the Santa Catalina Basin, off the coast of California, when they found the carcass of a gray whale. It contained the usual scavengers, such as hagfish, sleeper sharks, rattails, and amphipods, but there were also mats of bacteria and clamshells among the whale's bones. Further research revealed that one type of bacterium broke down fats, producing hydrogen sulphide.

Another bacterium, similar to those at vents, utilized the chemical to make food. They, in turn, provided food for other animals on the carcass, such as clams.

DNA tests

Examination of **DNA** from clams on the whale carcass showed it to be remarkably similar to clam DNA from hydrothermal vents. In addition, the scientists have found 10 different species on marine organisms that appear on both whale carcasses and at hydrothermal vents.

▲ *Dog whelks, starfish, urchins, and other deep-sea scavengers feed on a crab* (Cancer pagurus) *carcass. The carcass might also be an "island" at the bottom of the sea, used by creatures to island-hop from one place to the next.*

Bridges and corridors

Dispersal can mean an organism abandoning its current home and moving out. It might actively seek an unoccupied territory or be forced to move because of a change in its environment, such as climate or overcrowding and competition. It might move passively, chancing upon a new place to live quite by accident. There are several ways in which an organism can disperse.

Land bridges

There were times in the past when sea levels fell and land was exposed. This created a

Bering Land Bridge

| Bering land bridge | 0   100 miles |
| | 0 100 kilometers |

During the past million years, several sea level fluctuations have seen land bridges connect North America with both South America and Asia. Many animals crossed the bridges to colonize new lands. On several occasions, about 50,000–12,000 years ago, people probably crossed from Asia to North America.

bridge over which land plants and animals could pass. It was a way in which an organism could cross what had previously been a watery barrier. In the northern hemisphere, the Bering Land Bridge connected Alaska and Siberia during the Pleistocene Ice Ages. It enabled people, as well as animals, such as mammoths and saber-toothed cats, to emigrate from Asia into North America. Some herbivores—such as camels—traveled the other way, from North America to Asia.

Dinosaurs on the move

This was not the first time a Bering Land Bridge had formed. Dinosaurs made similar journeys about 70 million years ago. *Saurolophus* was a duck-bill dinosaur with a crest on the back of its head. Its fossils are found in both Mongolia and North America, the result of an emigration from North America to Asia. The ancestors of *Tyrannosaurus rex* were heading in the opposite direction. They had their origins in Asia but at some point they moved to North America.

Filter bridges

The Bering Land Bridge had two-way traffic, but animals that had their origins in South America did not cross it. They moved across another bridge, at the Isthmus of Panama, into North America but no further. Similarly, animals that had their origins in Asia did not move into South America. It is thought the Bering and Panama land bridges were too distant. Thus, the ecology in each area was so different from the conditions

Giant pandas live in relatively isolated groups. There are no natural corridors, through farmland, along which they can travel from one panda habitat to the next. This makes them vulnerable to any changes in their immediate environment.

the animals were familiar with, it prevented some species from dispersing any further. This type of bridge, where it is not certain who or what is going to cross, is known as a filter bridge.

ICE BRIDGE

About 8,000 years ago, an ice bridge connected the island of Öland with the Swedish mainland. It was over this temporary bridge that the first hunter-gatherers (the Alby people) colonized the island. They built huts on the shores of a prehistoric lagoon.

Corridors

Two places connected on a land mass make up a corridor. For example, in agricultural land in the United Kingdom, wildlife, such as wood mice and voles, has a preference for moving along hedges rather than across open fields. The hedges are dispersal corridors. The absence of corridors is a factor limiting the current distribution and survival of giant pandas in the wild in China. The panda's habitat is so fragmented there are no corridors to connect isolated populations. This means that when its main food plant, the bamboo, flowers and dies back in one area, the panda cannot disperse to other areas where the bamboo is still flourishing.

The Great American Interchange

On several occasions in the recent past, a land bridge has appeared and disappeared at the Isthmus of Panama, between North and South America. About 3 million years ago, there was a peak of activity on the bridge and it had a dramatic effect on the wildlife living on both continents. The bridge itself created a corridor through which North American species could disperse south into South America, and South American species could disperse north into North America.

Heading south

Camels, mastodons, tapirs, and horses were in the great wave of North American animals that entered South America. There were also powerful predators. For South American marsupials, the invasion was catastrophic. The incoming predators, such as cougars and saber-toothed cats, were more successful than the resident marsupial and large bird predators and many became extinct. These new predators also killed many of the large herbivores. However, many rodent and monkey species escaped.

Heading north

South America's smaller marsupials dispersed into Central and North America. Some, such as the Virginia opossum, reached as far north as the Canadian border with the United States. Large avian predators, such as terror birds, may have been going extinct in South America, but some pushed into North America for a short time. Other South American residents joined them. The South American armadillo had evolved an armored shell and the sloth had vicious, razor-sharp

Movement between North and South America

Pig family
Horse family
Camel family
Elephant family
Dog family
Bear family

NORTH AMERICA

ATLANTIC OCEAN

PACIFIC OCEAN

Anteater family
Sloth family
Armadillo family
Porcupine family
Opossum family

SOUTH AMERICA

0   500   1,000 miles
0   500   1,000 kilometers

Large numbers of animals, from many different animal groups, moved north or south across the Isthmus of Panama land bridge. They permanently changed the ecology of both North and South America.

claws so they were more than a match for the invaders from the north. The porcupine had its defensive quills. All three were part of the migration of South American species into North America. Ground sloth remains have been found in Florida and some species, such as *Megalonyx*, dispersed as far north as Alaska.

Dispersal and vicariance

The Panama land bridge also illustrates two basic principles in biogeography—dispersal and **vicariance**. Dispersal biogeography accounts for migration across barriers. It increases the distribution of a species. Vicariance biogeography is concerned with the barriers that arise and disrupt a species' distribution. The land bridge enabled a migration of terrestrial animals between North and South America—a case of dispersal. It also placed a barrier between

populations of marine organisms in the Gulf of Mexico and the Pacific Ocean—a case of vicariance. As a result, we find pairs of similar marine species living on either side of the bridge. Before the bridge arose they were each a single species.

PLACENTAL AND MARSUPIAL MAMMALS

During the Great American Interchange, two types of mammals were involved—placental and marsupial. Saber-toothed cats from North America and ground sloths from South America were placental mammals. Placental mammal females carry their babies in a womb and give birth to well-developed young. Opossums from South America are marsupials. Marsupial females have a pouch in which their infants develop (see page 22).

In the New World, terror birds were one of the main predators of the evolving horses.

Stepping stones

A string of islands may not form a solid land bridge, but they can create a route of stepping stones along which active dispersers, such as birds and mammals, can migrate. Whether an individual makes the journey depends on how close together the islands are. Visual predators, such as eagles, must be able to see the next stepping stone before they set off for the next island. For most species, though, it is simply a matter of chance.

Sweepstakes

Rare chance events that cause accidental dispersals are known as sweepstakes. Island-hopping and rafting are two methods of dispersal that fall into this category. The most recent invasions of Madagascar are thought to have been via a sweepstake route. Tenrecs, lemurs, fossas, mice, and pigmy hippos (now extinct) either rafted or swam from mainland Africa. Shrews, small monkeys, and small cats might have been the right size and shape to make such a journey but failed. They were,

SOUTH AMERICAN INVASION

Around 30 million years ago, South America was much closer to Africa than it is today. It is thought that members of at least two groups (rodents and primates) island-hopped from Africa to the northeast corner of Brazil. They drifted on rafts or floating islands. Estimates vary, but at that time a floating island with **stowaways** on board would have taken about 14.7 days with a favorable **paleowind**. Rodents and primates probably could have survived without water for up to 15 days, so they could just about make it to land before they died. Some must have made it, and some could have been pregnant females. The rodents established themselves in South America giving rise to capybaras, guinea pigs, viscachas, chinchillas, and New World porcupines. The monkeys evolved into the distinctive New World monkeys, including marmosets, tamarins, capuchins, uakaris, titis, and howler monkeys.

One theory states that rodents and monkeys island-hopped or rafted from Africa to South America when the continents were closer. An alternative theory holds that New World monkeys evolved from North American lemur-like primates, and they island- hopped through the Caribbean from North to South America.

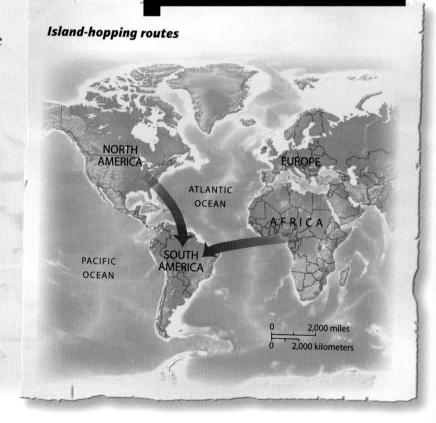

Island-hopping routes

as biogeographer George Gaylord Simpson (1902–1984) put it, "disappointed ticket-holders." Lions, elephants, apes, antelopes, and zebra did not even have "tickets." They were unlikely to swim or raft to the island. This accounts for the absence of monkeys, cats, and antelopes on Madagascar, even though the island is so close to Africa.

Caribbean island-hop

It is thought that animals inhabiting Caribbean islands in the island arc from Grenada, in the south, to the Virgin Islands, in the north, island-hopped and rafted through the chain from South America. In 1995, a bunch of green iguanas did just that. Ellen J. Censky, at the University of Oklahoma, is watching what happens next. At least 15 iguanas were cast adrift from Guadeloupe following Hurricanes Luis and Marilyn, in September 1995. After three weeks at sea, they were washed ashore on a tangle of huge uprooted trees about 200 miles (320 km) away on the island of Anguilla. Until then, Anguilla had no green iguanas. So scientists are now watching the immigrants to see if in their isolation they evolve into a new species.

Following a flood, these vine snails have clambered aboard a floating tree stump, which—in turn—acts as an island. Early animals may have traveled from one landmass to another in a similar way.

SURTSEY

On November 14, 1963, an underwater volcano pushed above the surface of the Atlantic Ocean, south of Iceland. The new island was named Surtsey in honor of Surtr, a mythical god in Nordic legend. The sea washed away ash from the first eruptions, but subsequent eruptions kept pace with erosion. By 1965, the new island had an area of 1 sq. mile (2.5 sq. km). Only scientists are permitted to visit so they can study how plants and animals colonize new land.

First arrivals

Flies flew in before the lava had cooled, some having been blown from as far away as Europe, and spiderlings ballooned over (see page 24). The first organisms to gain a hold were mosses and lichens. The first higher plant was sea rocket, followed by sea lyme grass, oyster plant, and sea sandwort. Their tough seeds were probably washed ashore from islands to the north. Sea sandwort has a root system that grows deep into the sand and utilizes nutrients from a wide area, making it

▲ To the south of Iceland, the volcanic island of Surtsey appeared over a geologically active zone in the ocean known as the Mid-Atlantic ridge. The eruption began 425 ft. (130 m) below sea level. It is named after the fire god Surtr, from Norse mythology.

one of the most successful plants to colonize the island. Today, it is the most common higher plant on the island—there are more than a million of them! By 1995, the first bush had grown. It was a dwarf willow, a common plant in Iceland. Its seeds were probably carried to Surtsey on the wind, and fertilizer in the form of seabird droppings helped germination. Later arrivals were tea-leaved willow and woolly willow, both hardy, low-growing shrubs.

Steady procession

Three years after the eruptions stopped, birds such as fulmars and guillemots arrived to nest. By 1985 a gull colony had been established. The gulls, more than any other bird species, brought life on their feet and their droppings helped to improve the soil. In 2003, a northern green orchid and lady's bedstraw germinated in the gull colony. Some organisms drifted ashore. In 1974, a grass **tussock** washed up. Half of it was taken for analysis. On board were more than 600 terrestrial invertebrates, mostly springtails and mites, most of them still alive. Likewise, floating driftwood has arrived loaded with insect stowaways, including spiders and beetles. The first earthworm was spotted in 1993 and the first slug in 1998. Both were probably carried over by birds from southern Iceland or nearby Heimaey.

Stopover site

Gray seals and harbor seals visited the island shortly after it appeared. Both species now crawl onto the shore to bask in the sun or give birth. They have attracted the attention of killer whales. The island is also the stop-off point for large swans and geese migrating between Iceland and the British Isles. Puffins also arrived and began breeding in 2004. By 2007, Surtsey had been reduced by wind, wave, and rain erosion to 0.5 sq. miles (1.4 sq km), about half its original size. But it is still an exciting living laboratory.

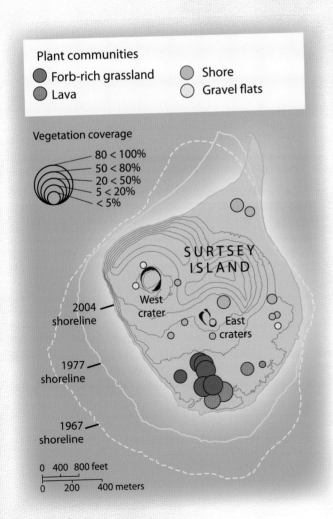

◀ Changing shape of Surtsey and its wildlife distribution

Permanent study plots on Surtsey show the pattern of plant communities in different parts of the island in 2004.

In the wrong place at the wrong time

In some parts of the world, fruit growers are relying more on natural predators and less on **pesticides** to control pests. One unexpected result was that black widow spiders turned up in bunches of grapes at British supermarkets. The spiders had crossed halfway across the world, well outside their normal distribution. It is an unnatural but common method of dispersal.

Jump dispersal

This movement of organisms across great distances is known as jump dispersal. Following it, descendants of the disperser will often establish a population. At least one of the supermarket's black widow spiders would have had to be carrying eggs. More usually, spiders disperse as spiderlings (see page 24). They spin a silken thread and are swept up into the air as if on a paraglider. In this way, spiderlings can cross great barriers, including oceans and mountain chains—a more natural form of jump dispersal.

Accidental introductions

Organisms carried by people can be dispersed accidentally or deliberately. Marine larvae carried in ships' ballast tanks are a particular concern. They are discharged into habitats where they can wreak havoc. Cargo ships without cargo take seawater into ballast tanks so the ship sits better in the water and steers more effectively. When cargo is about to be taken on, the tanks are pumped out. The place where the water is taken in is usually different than where it is pumped out. Therefore, marine organisms from one place are transported to another. Zebra mussels have spread this way, into the Great Lakes and other waterways where they out-competed native species.

Cane toads are up to 6 in. (15 cm) long. Both adults and tadpoles are poisonous. They eat dead and living matter and have become so successful that they are a pest species in Australia. They were originally introduced to control pests.

ACCLIMATIZATION SOCIETY

In the 19th century, acclimatization societies sprang up all over the world. One object was for settlers in foreign countries to import familiar animals from their homeland. They especially introduced game animals for hunting and shooting. Sometimes the introduction was catastrophic. The introduction of rabbits to Australia was the main reason 12 percent of native mammals there became extinct.

One of the strangest introductions was by Eugene Schieffelin, of the American Acclimatization Society. He wanted to release all the species of birds mentioned in Shakespeare's plays into the United States. He started with 60 starlings in New York's Central Park. Now, there are 200 million starlings in the United States! They are a pest species everywhere.

In Europe, Chinese mitten crabs have invaded **estuaries** where they threaten the stability of river banks.

Deliberate introductions

Alien species are sometimes introduced deliberately to places where it is thought they might do some good. Generally, the opposite happens. In 1935, the cane or marine toad was introduced to Australia from the Americas to control the native cane grub. It was considered a safer way to control the pest than using pesticides. However, the toad became so successful it has now overrun parts of Queensland, eliminating local competitors. In its natural home, on the shores of South America, there are no more than 20 adult toads to be found along every 330 ft. (100 m) of shoreline. In Queensland, there are up to 2,000 toads! The pest catcher has become a pest itself.

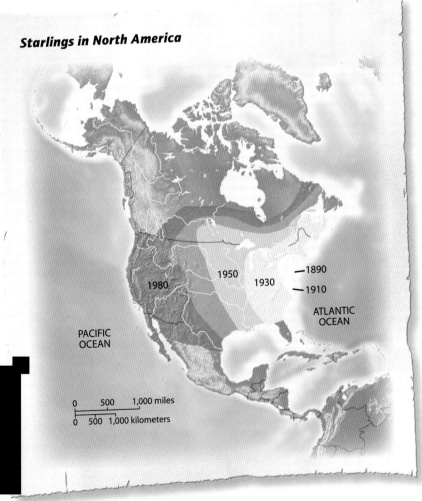

Starlings in North America

1950   1930   — 1890
1980   — 1910

ATLANTIC OCEAN

PACIFIC OCEAN

0   500   1,000 miles
0   500   1,000 kilometers

Sixty European starlings were released in Central Park, New York, in 1890 and another 40 in 1891. They spread all over North America. Unfortunately, starlings drive native birds, such as bluebirds and purple martins, away from nesting sites.

Danger: killer bees!

In May 1991, Jesus Diaz was mowing his lawn in Brownsville, Texas, when a swarm of bees attacked him. He was stung about 18 times, was hospitalized, and lived. He was the first person in the United States to be attacked by killer bees. These especially aggressive honeybees were bred from African and European honeybees and taken to an experimental station in Brazil to create a hybrid bee that produced more honey. In 1957, a swarm escaped. The bees dispersed gradually northward toward Central America, at a rate of 200 miles (320 km) a year. The bees crossed the Isthmus of Panama and reached the United States in 1990. This steady expansion of their range is known as diffusion. This is the gradual movement of a population of plants or animals through a favorable habitat during the course of many generations. In this case, the killer bee queens mate with local drones and new colonies establish gradually further away from the accidental release site. These bees tend to swarm more frequently than normal honeybees, so they spread relatively quickly. They are very defensive and have killed several people, not because their venom is so potent, but because they attack in such large numbers.

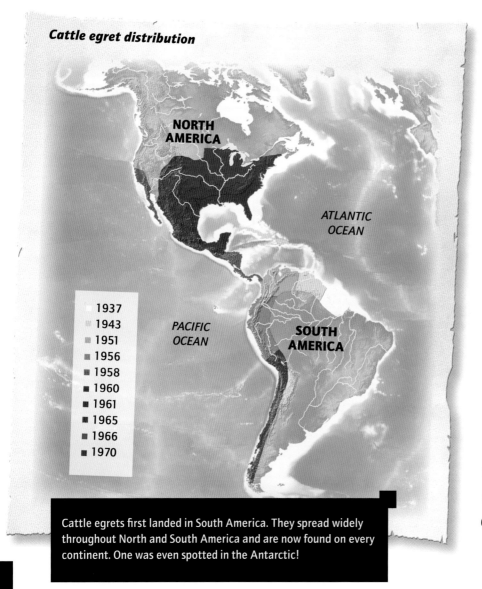

Cattle egret distribution

1937
1943
1951
1956
1958
1960
1961
1965
1966
1970

NORTH AMERICA

ATLANTIC OCEAN

PACIFIC OCEAN

SOUTH AMERICA

Cattle egrets first landed in South America. They spread widely throughout North and South America and are now found on every continent. One was even spotted in the Antarctic!

Under their own steam

Since the late 19th century, an enterprising bird has undertaken a similar but less alarming dispersal. The invader is the cattle egret, a small white heron that lives in grassy habitats. It is native to Africa, but appeared on the Courantyne River, Suriname, on the northeast coast of South America, in 1877.

By the 1930s, it had started to disperse further afield, another case of diffusion migration.

By the 1970s, it was distributed from Argentina to the U.S.-Canadian border. Amazingly, humans did not introduce the bird to the New World. It flew itself—all the way across the Atlantic Ocean!

Gradually evolve

Today, the distribution of the camel family in both the Old and New World's looks remarkably similar to the distribution of marsupials and ratites (see page 22). Continental drift, however, is not the reason. The camels were part of the Great American Interchange (see page 30). They originated in North America, emigrated south across the Panama land bridge to South America, and east across the Bering land bridge to Asia. The expansion of their range was over such a long time period that the environments to which they moved changed through time. Some camels were suited to the new conditions and survived, while others were not and became extinct. **Natural selection** was acting on successive generations and this gave rise to new species, such as guanacos and vicuñas in South America, and dromedary and Bactrian camels in Africa and Asia. This extremely slow migration, during which many evolutionary changes occur, is known as secular migration.

The Middle Eastern dromedary, Asian Bactrian camel, and their South American relatives, descended from ancestors that lived in North America. They migrated across land bridges to their current positions.

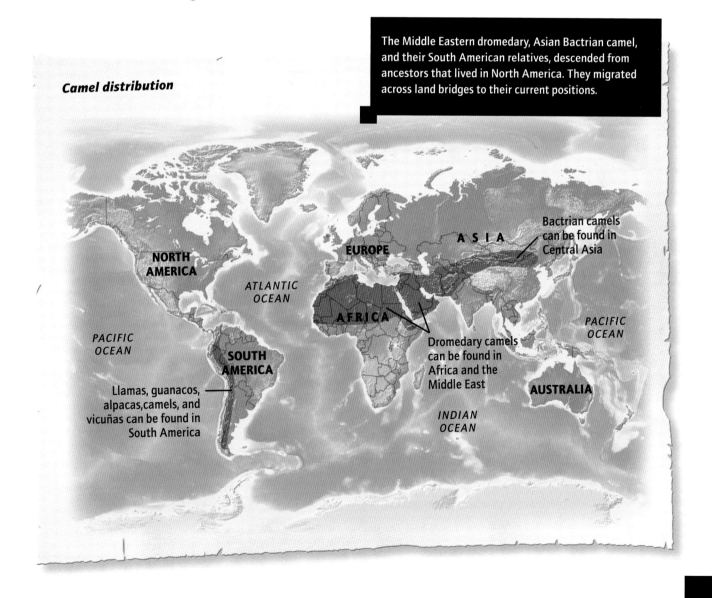

Camel distribution

NORTH AMERICA

EUROPE

ASIA

Bactrian camels can be found in Central Asia

ATLANTIC OCEAN

AFRICA

PACIFIC OCEAN

PACIFIC OCEAN

SOUTH AMERICA

Llamas, guanacos, alpacas, camels, and vicuñas can be found in South America

Dromedary camels can be found in Africa and the Middle East

AUSTRALIA

INDIAN OCEAN

SPECIES
DISTRIBUTION

The geographic range of a species is the limit to where its population lives. For example, polar bears are confined to the Arctic. Within this range there may be small or large concentrations of individuals. The number of individuals in any one place is determined by where suitable habitat is found and by whether individuals prefer to live together with others of their own kind or alone. Species distribution, therefore, is the way in which groups of **organisms** in a population are spread out. There are three types of distribution: clumped; uniform; and random.

Clumped distribution

Wolf packs live in large territories. Each territory is separated from its neighbor by a buffer zone, a no-go area in which the wolves rarely venture. Wolves patrol their boundaries regularly. They scent mark trees and bushes with chemical markers (such as urine) that tell other wolf packs to keep out. In this way they can keep prey living in their territory to themselves. This kind of local distribution is referred to as clumped. It is the most common type of distribution pattern. It is seen in places where resources, such as food, are

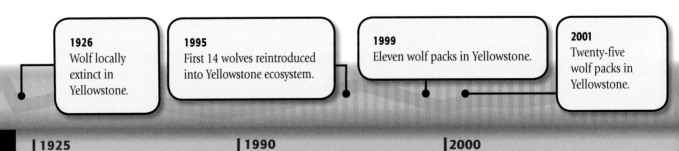

1926	1995	1999	2001
Wolf locally extinct in Yellowstone.	First 14 wolves reintroduced into Yellowstone ecosystem.	Eleven wolf packs in Yellowstone.	Twenty-five wolf packs in Yellowstone.

| 1925 | 1990 | 2000 |

concentrated in small areas within the animal's home range. For example, wolf prey, such as elk, tend to live in small herds.

The type of soil determines the local distribution of plants. For example, the eastern red cedar of North America is usually found on limestone outcrops. Sphagnum moss grows in acidic, boggy conditions, and marram grass is exclusive to coastal sand dunes.

Microclimates, such as those under a log, determine where slugs or woodlice might live—hidden places where there is high humidity. Social factors might also influence distribution. Elephant seals come onto land at the same time on specific breeding beaches to mate and give birth to their calves. Going to the same beaches at the same time means that they will meet a partner. Great white sharks gather offshore to catch the seals when they re-enter the water. These are both examples of clumped distribution.

Uniform distribution

Several species of penguin, tern, and gull nest in large and noisy colonies. Each bird has its own space and is a set distance from its neighbor (usually the distance it can peck while still on the nest). Certain plants, such as the rhododendron and bracken, produce chemicals that prevent other species of plants from growing nearby. Creosote bushes tend to be spaced out evenly in the desert, so that each ensures it has sufficient moisture. Humans often show a uniform distribution when sunbathing on a beach. Uniform distribution is often the result of how closely a neighbor can be tolerated.

Random distribution

Plants with wind-borne seeds, such as dandelions, are said to have a random distribution. Their seeds are at the mercy of the wind. The larvae of marine creatures (such as crabs, lobsters, and coral polyps) float away on ocean currents. In spring, all corals **spawn** at exactly the same time on the Great Barrier Reef. The mass spawning is like an upside-down snowstorm. The resulting larvae drift away, starting new coral reefs wherever they settle.

Yellowstone wolf distribution

Yellowstone's wolf packs are each given a name relating to the place where they patrol a well-guarded territory.

2002
Druid Peak Pack of 37 wolves splits into three new packs.

2004
Last of the reintroduced Yellowstone wolves die.

2005
Number of wolves in Yellowstone declines by 31 percent.

2006
Wolf distribution in Yellowstone changed very little.

| 2002 | 2004 | 2006 |

Fight to survive

Organisms are rarely alone. They interact not only with others of their own kind but also with individuals from other species. These interactions are factors that influence where an organism lives and its relative abundance.

Protoco-operation

Africa's honey badger—a mammal—has a surprising relationship with a bird called the honeyguide. The bird encourages the badger to follow it to bees' nests, by flying around conspicuously and calling loudly. The two animals gain from each other's behavior. The honeyguide is good at finding bees' nests but less good at opening them. The honey badger is less good at finding them but very good at ripping them apart to get at the grubs and honey. This kind of relationship, in which two species interact for mutual benefit, but do not depend on each other entirely, is called protoco-operation.

Mutualism

Mutualism is a type of relationship that is vital for much of life on the land. About 90 percent of land plants rely on a close association with a mycorrhizal fungus. The fungus absorbs nutrients from the soil more efficiently than the plant's roots, then passes them to the plant. The plant, in return, provides the fungus with sugars that it has manufactured through **photosynthesis**. Both benefit from the relationship.

Commensalism

Commensalism is a relationship in which only one organism gains but the other is unaffected. When a hummingbird thrusts its bill into a blossom to sip nectar, a procession of mites clambers on or off the bird's beak. The mites use the birds to travel between flowers. The bird is unaware of, and unaffected by, the mite transportation service it is providing.

The female mosquito is a blood predator. She needs blood to help her eggs develop. On most occasions the prey is not killed, only irritated. However, in the Arctic there are so many mosquitoes that a caribou calf can die from loss of blood. The male mosquito drinks mainly nectar.

Predation

Predation is when one organism (predator) feeds on another organism (prey). An organism can be both predator and prey, e.g. a bird catches an insect but is grabbed by a snake. True predation means the prey is either swallowed whole, like a dolphin swallowing a fish, or is chewed, like a lion feasting on a wildebeest. Plants are not immune, since seed predators eat and destroy the seeds. Grazers, such as wildebeest and zebra, do not kill their prey. These herbivores trim leaves but do not destroy the plant. **Parasites** are a type of grazer that do not kill their host. Female mosquitoes graze blood from their victim, but do not kill it. Parasitoids, on the other hand, feed on their host and eventually kill it. Ichneumon wasps, for example, lay their eggs on caterpillars. Their larvae feed on their caterpillar hosts until they eventually die.

Competition

When resources are limited, organisms compete with each other. Those resources could be food, water, sunlight, territory, or a partner.

The snake is a predator and the mouse prey, but the snake could also be prey if it is spotted by an eagle.

INTERACTIONS BETWEEN ORGANISMS

Interaction	Species A	Species B	Effect
Neutralism	No change	No change	Populations do not affect each other—rare
Protoco-operation	Gain	Gain	Both gain but the relationship is not permanent
Mutualism	Gain	Gain	Both gain and the relationship is essential
Commensalism	Gain	No change	A (commensal) gains but B (host) gains nothing
Competition	Lose	Lose	Both hinder each other
Predation	Gain	Lose	A eats B

Competition can occur within and between species. In a tropical rain forest, plants compete vigorously for light. The tree canopy is so dense with leaves and branches that little light reaches the forest floor. A tall tree has a distinct competitive advantage over a smaller tree.

Populations on the move

Migration is the two-way movement of animals, often between seasonal breeding and feeding sites. In the deep-sea, there is a daily, vertical migration of small fish from the twilight zone, where they spend the day, to surface waters, where they feed at night. It is known as diel (or diurnal) migration, and is an adaptation to avoid predators that rely on sight to find their prey. However, some predators, such as small deep-sea sharks, make the same daily journey!

Regular routes

Many migrants follow traditional routes. Bird migrants follow regular flyways, but their predictable path makes them vulnerable to predators. Predators even adapt their breeding cycles to coincide with times of plenty. Eleonora's falcons, in the southern

GREEN TURTLES OF ASCENSION ISLAND

One population of Brazil's green sea turtles feed on the coast. These beaches would be perfectly suitable for breeding on but the turtles leave them, head into the Atlantic, and swim to Ascension Island to lay their eggs. Why they go has given rise to a heated debate. Scientists that believe in a **vicariance hypothesis**, suggest that when the Atlantic was much narrower (about 70 million years ago) the turtles did not have to go so far. As the ocean widened, at a rate of 0.8 in. (2 cm) a year, the turtles continued to follow their instinct and go back to the beach they were born on. Through successive generations, the gap they swam became increasingly wider. Today it is more than 1,250 miles (2,000 km) wide! Scientists who propose a **dispersal hypothesis** argue that the turtles have simply gone there in more recent times. In 1989, Brian Bowen, at the University of Georgia, examined DNA from turtles that journeyed to Ascension Island and those that remained at several Brazilian nesting sites. He found the origins of the migration must have been relatively recent. So the dispersal argument seems to be closer to the truth.

Migration to Ascension Island

The map shows the routes taken by five green turtles. They were tracked by satellite during their migration from Brazil to Ascension Island. How they find their way is a mystery. At more than 3.3 ft. (1 m) long, Ascension Island turtles are some of the largest green turtles in the world.

Mediterranean, delay having chicks until the fall, when they intercept small birds on their southward migration to Africa.

journey between southern Canada in summer and Mexico in winter is a 4,000 mile (6,500 km) round trip!

Great distances

Migration distances vary enormously. A frog spends most of the year close to a pond. At breeding time, it dives in to attract a mate. Its migration can be measured in feet. The Arctic tern, however, spends half the year in the Arctic where it breeds and the other half in the Antarctic where its feeds. It has an annual round trip of 24,000 miles (38,000 km). The longest migration undertaken by a mammal is that of the gray whale. Its annual journey, between breeding sites in Baja California and feeding sites in the Bering Sea, is up to 14,000 miles (22,000 km). One of the longest insect migrations is that of the monarch butterfly. Its

Short distances

In Jellyfish Lake, on the island of Palau to the east of the Philippines, thousands of jellyfish migrate each day, from one side to the other. They harbor green algae. The algae have a safe place to live and the jellyfish obtain nutrients from the algae. The algae need sunlight to photosynthesize. So the jellyfish ensure they have maximum sun exposure by migrating across the lake and staying out of the shade. At night, the jellyfish make another migration. On the bottom of the lake is a stagnant area on top of which bacteria grow. The jellyfish sink down to the bacteria to feed some more. In the morning they return to the surface and the sun.

Sea turtles migrate vast distances across the oceans, traveling between breeding and feeding sites. The females come onto land to deposit their eggs in a hole they dig in the sand.

Dinosaur migration

Scientists have recently proven that birds are the living descendants of dinosaurs. So, if birds migrate, why didn't dinosaurs? Clues may be found in fossilized dinosaur tracks. Martin Lockley, at the University of Colorado, has been studying them. He suggests that large, plant-eating dinosaurs, such as hadrosaurs (duck-billed dinosaurs) and iguanodontids, were social animals and traveled in large herds, just as buffalo do today. They probably spread out over large areas while foraging for food. There is evidence to suggest that some of those that spent part of the year in colder latitudes, such as Alaska, did migrate south to warmer temperatures in winter.

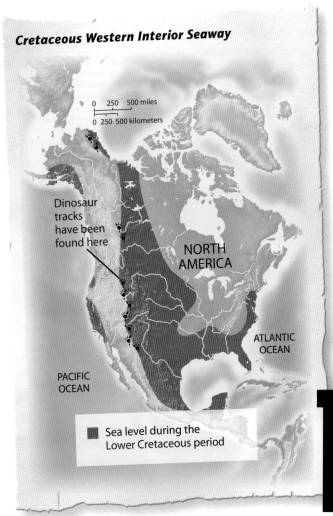

Cretaceous Western Interior Seaway

0   250   500 miles

0   250 500 kilometers

Dinosaur tracks have been found here

NORTH AMERICA

ATLANTIC OCEAN

PACIFIC OCEAN

■ Sea level during the Lower Cretaceous period

Dinosaur highway

About 100 million years ago, a shallow sea—the Cretaceous Western Interior Seaway—divided North America from the Arctic Ocean to the Gulf of Mexico. It was about where the Great Plains are today. The Dakota sandstones, which are made of ancient, shallow river and seashore deposits, contain many tracks made by dinosaurs and ancient crocodiles. At Dinosaur Ridge, Colorado, and Clayton Lakes, New Mexico, the dinosaur tracks are of large, three-toed *ornithopods*, probably iguanodontids. There are also the smaller tracks of meat-eating, *theropod* dinosaurs. At Mosquero Creek, New Mexico, 55 parallel trackways show a herd of small ornithopod dinosaurs heading north. At the same site, 10 parallel tracks of larger ornithopods indicate a group heading south. Paleontologists have found so many dinosaur tracks in this area that it is believed to have been a migration highway, where dinosaurs journeyed north and south along the western shores of the shallow sea.

Going home

What if the dinosaur's journeys were seasonal? Did the dinosaurs have any idea where "home" might be and return there, as bird migrants do today? Evidence to suggest that they might have comes from research done in Australia by Mark Read and colleagues, at Queensland

The Cretaceous Western Interior Seaway was filled with water when dinosaurs dominated the Earth. Rocks that would have been laid down on the western shore of the sea contain the fossilized footprints of dinosaurs. They indicate that some dinosaurs were seasonal migrants.

Parks and Wildlife Service, Australia Zoo, and the University of Queensland. They began a satellite-tracking program with saltwater crocodiles, the world's largest living reptiles. Crocodiles were caught and shipped by helicopter to release points at set distances from where they were caught. All of the crocs found their way home. One crocodile traveled more than 250 miles (400 km) in 20 days. If modern crocodiles have this homing ability, then maybe ancient dinosaurs did, too!

Each species of dinosaur, like most other animals, might have been able to survive in several types of habitat. But they would not have been able to create sufficient changes to survive in a totally alien environment. Only humans can do that. With ingenuity and technology, people can live just about anywhere. It could mean that one day the distribution of humans will not be confined to planet Earth!

Fossilized trackways with sauropod footprints indicate that herds probably went on migrations to find more lush vegetation during hot, dry spells. The largest sauropod trackway (with 10,000 footprints) was found at Nashville, Arkansas,.

TIMELINE

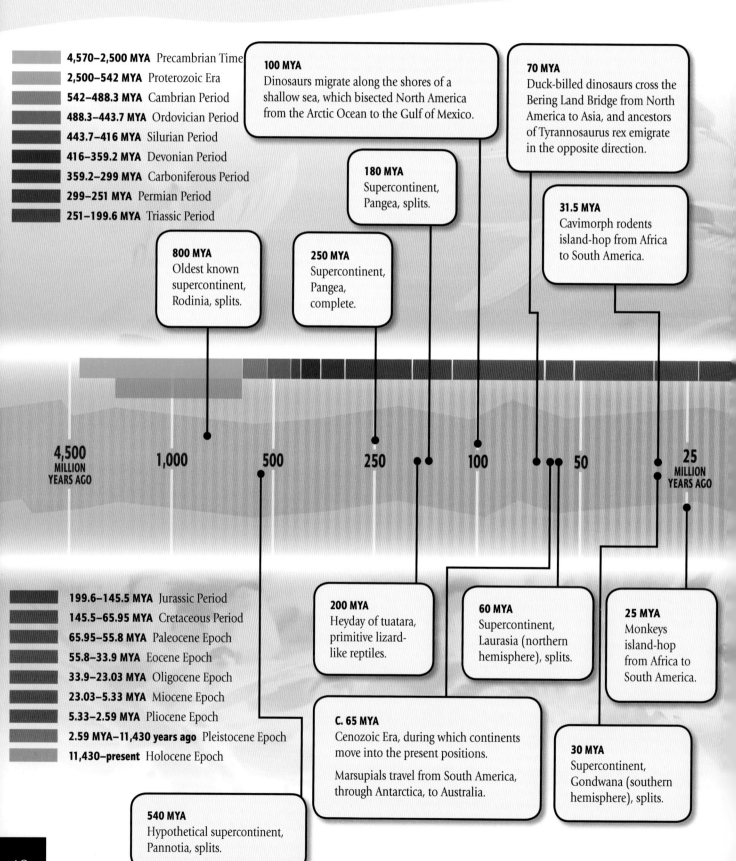

4,570–2,500 MYA Precambrian Time
2,500–542 MYA Proterozoic Era
542–488.3 MYA Cambrian Period
488.3–443.7 MYA Ordovician Period
443.7–416 MYA Silurian Period
416–359.2 MYA Devonian Period
359.2–299 MYA Carboniferous Period
299–251 MYA Permian Period
251–199.6 MYA Triassic Period

100 MYA
Dinosaurs migrate along the shores of a shallow sea, which bisected North America from the Arctic Ocean to the Gulf of Mexico.

70 MYA
Duck-billed dinosaurs cross the Bering Land Bridge from North America to Asia, and ancestors of Tyrannosaurus rex emigrate in the opposite direction.

180 MYA
Supercontinent, Pangea, splits.

31.5 MYA
Cavimorph rodents island-hop from Africa to South America.

800 MYA
Oldest known supercontinent, Rodinia, splits.

250 MYA
Supercontinent, Pangea, complete.

4,500 MILLION YEARS AGO

1,000

500

250

100

50

25 MILLION YEARS AGO

199.6–145.5 MYA Jurassic Period
145.5–65.95 MYA Cretaceous Period
65.95–55.8 MYA Paleocene Epoch
55.8–33.9 MYA Eocene Epoch
33.9–23.03 MYA Oligocene Epoch
23.03–5.33 MYA Miocene Epoch
5.33–2.59 MYA Pliocene Epoch
2.59 MYA–11,430 years ago Pleistocene Epoch
11,430–present Holocene Epoch

200 MYA
Heyday of tuatara, primitive lizard-like reptiles.

60 MYA
Supercontinent, Laurasia (northern hemisphere), splits.

25 MYA
Monkeys island-hop from Africa to South America.

C. 65 MYA
Cenozoic Era, during which continents move into the present positions.

Marsupials travel from South America, through Antarctica, to Australia.

30 MYA
Supercontinent, Gondwana (southern hemisphere), splits.

540 MYA
Hypothetical supercontinent, Pannotia, splits.

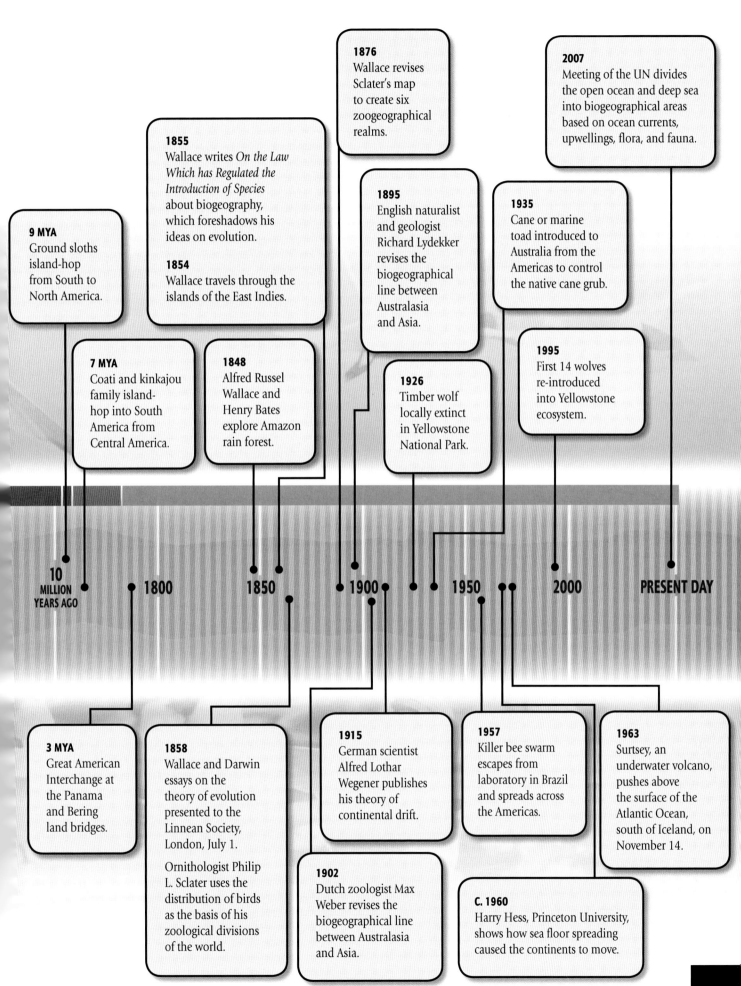

1876
Wallace revises Sclater's map to create six zoogeographical realms.

2007
Meeting of the UN divides the open ocean and deep sea into biogeographical areas based on ocean currents, upwellings, flora, and fauna.

1855
Wallace writes *On the Law Which has Regulated the Introduction of Species* about biogeography, which foreshadows his ideas on evolution.

1854
Wallace travels through the islands of the East Indies.

1895
English naturalist and geologist Richard Lydekker revises the biogeographical line between Australasia and Asia.

1935
Cane or marine toad introduced to Australia from the Americas to control the native cane grub.

9 MYA
Ground sloths island-hop from South to North America.

7 MYA
Coati and kinkajou family island-hop into South America from Central America.

1848
Alfred Russel Wallace and Henry Bates explore Amazon rain forest.

1926
Timber wolf locally extinct in Yellowstone National Park.

1995
First 14 wolves re-introduced into Yellowstone ecosystem.

10 MILLION YEARS AGO   **1800**   **1850**   **1900**   **1950**   **2000**   **PRESENT DAY**

3 MYA
Great American Interchange at the Panama and Bering land bridges.

1858
Wallace and Darwin essays on the theory of evolution presented to the Linnean Society, London, July 1.

Ornithologist Philip L. Sclater uses the distribution of birds as the basis of his zoological divisions of the world.

1915
German scientist Alfred Lothar Wegener publishes his theory of continental drift.

1957
Killer bee swarm escapes from laboratory in Brazil and spreads across the Americas.

1963
Surtsey, an underwater volcano, pushes above the surface of the Atlantic Ocean, south of Iceland, on November 14.

1902
Dutch zoologist Max Weber revises the biogeographical line between Australasia and Asia.

C. 1960
Harry Hess, Princeton University, shows how sea floor spreading caused the continents to move.

FIND OUT MORE

Further reading

Burnie, David. *Animal: The Definitive Visual Guide to the World's Wildlife.* New York: DK Publishing, 2005.

Davis, Barbara. *Biomes and Ecosystems.* Milwaukee, Wis.: Gareth Stevens, 2007.

Landau, Elaine. *Killer Bees: Fearsome, Scary and Creepy Animals.* Berkeley Heights, N. J.: Enslow, 2003.

Cheung, Catherine, Lyndon DeVantier and Kay Van Damme. *Socotra: a Natural History of the Islands and their People.* New York: W. W. Morton, 2007.

Websites

Find out more about some of the organizations mentioned in the text:

Bryn Mawr College
http://www.brynmawr.edu

The Linnean Society of London
http://www.linnean.org/

University of California, Santa Barbara
http://www.ucsb.edu

Queensland Parks and Wildlife Service
http://www.epa.qld.gov.au

General reference sites

The following websites will take you further into the subject of evolution and biodiversity.

University of California Museum of Paleontology
http://www.ucmp.berkeley.edu/index.php

University of California at Berkeley
http://evolution.berkeley.edu/evolibrary/home.php

London's Natural History Museum
http://www.nhm.ac.uk

New York's American Museum of Natural History
http://www.amnh.org

Smithsonian Institution
http://www.si.edu

Chicago's The Field Museum
http://www.fieldmuseum.org

Biology news

News of new developments in life sciences can be found at:

http://www.pbs.org/wgbh/nova/
sciencenow/involved/news.html

http://www.sciencedaily.com

http://sciencenow.sciencemag.org

http://www.newscientist.com/news.ns

To research

Find out more about great white sharks and their migrations.

How big are these sharks? What do they eat? Where are they usually seen? Where do they travel to and why? Take a look here:

http://www.tunaresearch.org/shark/
    research.html

http://topp.org

http://ims.ucsc.edu

Learn more about long-distance traveler Nicole:

http://www.whitesharktrust.org/
    migration.html

Read about great white sharks in:

Markle, Sandra. *Great White Sharks (Animal Predators)*. Minneapolis, Minn.: Carolrhoda Books, 2004.

For a real life adventure with great white sharks read:

Matthiessen, Peter. *Blue Meridian: the Search for the Great White Shark.* New York: Random House, 1973.

or watch:

Blue Water White Death (MGM, 2007)

Go deep with "Alvin."

Find out more about the deep-sea submersible "Alvin" at:

http://www.whoi.edu

and read about it:

Matsen, Bradford. *The Incredible Submersible Alvin Discovers a Strange Deep-Sea World*. New York: Enslow Publishers, 2003.

Find out more about the island of Socotra.

Was it once a part of Africa or the Middle East? What is so special about its plants and animals? Check out:

http://socotraisland.org

Find out more about deep-sea hydrothermal vents.

Where in the world are they to be found? How many different types of vents are there? What animals live close to vents?

http://www.resa.net/nasa/
    ocean_hydrothermal.htm

What is NeMO?

Try looking here:

http://www.pmel.noaa.gov/vents/nemo

Go on a "Voyage to the Deep" here:

http://www.ocean.udel.edu/deepsea

Find out more about Surtsey.

What is the volcano doing now? How many new animal visitors have arrived and which ones have stayed? Start looking here:

http://www.surtsey.is/index_eng.htm

http://denali.gsfc.nasa.gov/research/
   garvin/surtsey.html

http://volcano.und.edu/vwdocs/volc_
images/europe_west_asia/surtsey.html

Find out more about the Bering Land Bridge.

How many times has it formed? Which animals crossed the bridge? When did they cross? Which way did they go, east or west? Watch an animation of the flooding of the Bering Land Bridge at:

http://www.ncdc.noaa.gov/paleo/parcs/
   atlas/beringia/lbridge.html

Find out about the historical and cultural significance of the Bering Land Bridge at:

http://www.nps.gov/bela/

http://beringlandbridge.areaparks.com

GLOSSARY

angiosperms flowering plants

archipelago group of islands

biodiversity hotspot place on Earth where there are an unusually large number of species

biomes specific places on Earth where climate, vegetation, and landscape produce the same conditions and similar environments

classification method by which scientists group and categorize different living things

colonize when one or more species populates a new area

cosmopolitan occurring in many different parts of the world

dispersal hypothesis proposal that organisms arise in a center of origin and spread out by stages, using corridors and by crossing or hopping over barriers. Which groups cross and when they cross is random.

DNA stands for deoxyribonucleic acid, which contains all the genetic instructions for the development and functioning of a living thing

ecology study of the interaction of living things and their environment

endemic species organisms that live exclusively in one part of the world

estuary semi-enclosed body of coastal water into which run rivers and streams

fauna animal life

feral refers to a plant or animal that was once domesticated but has returned to the wild

flora plant life

hybrid offspring resulting from crossbreeding different species of plants or animals

hypothesis tentative explanation for a phenomenon or event, while a theory is an explanation based on a wealth of data

microclimate locality in which the climate differs from the surrounding area, e.g. a city street where the temperature is higher than the surrounding countryside

microinch one microinch is the same as one thousandth of an inch

micro-organism living thing that cannot be seen by the naked eye so has to be observed through a microscope

natural selection process by which favorable inherited characteristics become more common and less favorable ones become less common in successive generations

naturalist person who studies natural history

niche functional position of a species or population of species in an ecosystem, which describes not only where it is but also what it does

oceanography study of the oceans and seas—the marine environment

organism individual living system, such as a plant, animal, bacterium, or fungi, that reacts to stimuli, reproduces, grows, and maintains itself

ornithologist person who studies birds

paleontologist person who studies fossils

paleowind ancient wind that blew thousands or even millions of years ago

parasite organism that lives on or inside another organism and causes it harm

permafrost layer of soil that is at or below freezing temperature all year round

pesticides chemicals used to kill pests, such as rats, aphids, and weeds

photosynthesis conversion of light energy from sunlight into chemical energy using carbon dioxide and water

plate tectonics theory in geology that explains the movements of landmasses and the ocean floor on Earth's surface

plateau area of high, flat land

remnant species plant or animal that remains behind when many of the other species that once lived in the ecosystem have moved elsewhere or become extinct

reptile four-limbed, air-breathing vertebrate animals that have their skin covered in scales

spawn eggs and sperm from animals such as fish and amphibians

spores reproductive body that algae, fungi, liverworts, mosses, lichens, ferns, and some protozoans use for dispersal and for long-term survival in unfavorable conditions

stowaways organisms that hitch a lift on other organisms without them knowing, much like a person traveling illegally on a bus, train, or boat

temperate in geography this refers to the lands between the tropics and polar regions

terrestrial anything that is of, on, or relating to Earth (e.g. a terrestrial animal is one that lives on land as opposed to in water, air, or trees)

theory of evolution notion, based on observable facts, that organisms developed by a process of gradual and continuous change from previously existing forms

tussock any grass that grows in tufts or clumps rather than in a uniform mat (also refers to a particular type of moth)

vicariance separation of organisms by a geographical barrier, which results in differentiation at either side of the barrier and can lead to the formation of new species

vicariance hypothesis proposal that the distribution of plants and animals depends on their normal means of dispersal. It means that any disruption to the continuous range of a species can be explained by the existence of new barriers, such as mountain building or sea level rise. Where there are sufficient similarities between two populations that probably once split, this hypothesis invokes the existence of land bridges and former continents to explain the pattern of dispersal.

zoogeographic pertaining to the geographic distribution of animal species

zoologist person who scientifically studies animals, focusing mainly upon structure, classification, and distribution

INDEX

DATE DUE

BRODART, CO.   Cat. No. 23-221